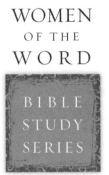

WOMEN
OF THE
WORD

BIBLE
STUDY
SERIES

A WOMAN
AFTER GOD'S
HEART

EADIE GOODBOY

Gospel Light

Published by Gospel Light
Ventura, California, U.S.A.
www.gospellight.com
Printed in the U.S.A.

Aglow International is an interdenominational organization of
Christian women. Our mission is to lead women to Jesus Christ and provide
opportunity for Christian women to grow in their faith and minister to others.
Our publications are used to help women find a personal relationship with
Jesus Christ, to enhance growth in their Christian experience, and to help them
recognize their roles and relationships according to Scripture. For more
information about our organization, please write to Aglow International,
P.O. Box 1749, Edmonds, WA 98020-1749, U.S.A., or call (425) 775-7282.
For ordering or information about the Aglow studies and other
resources, visit the Aglow E-store at www.aglow.org.

Rights for publishing this book outside the U.S.A. or in non-English languages are
administered by Gospel Light Worldwide, an international not-for-profit ministry.
For additional information, please visit www.glww.org, email info@glww.org, or write
to Gospel Light Worldwide, 1957 Eastman Avenue, Ventura, CA 93003, U.S.A.

To order copies of this book and other Gospel Light products in bulk quantities,
please contact us at 1-800-446-7735.

CONTENTS

FOREWORD

When the apostle Paul poured out his heart in letters to the young churches in Asia, he was responding to his apostolic call to shepherd those tender flocks. They needed encouragement in their new life in Jesus. They needed solid doctrine. They needed truth from someone who had an intimate relationship with God and with them.

Did Paul know as he was writing that these simple letters would form the bulk of the New Testament? We can be confident that the Holy Spirit did! How like God to use Paul's relationship with these churches to cement His plan and purpose in their lives, and, generations later, in ours.

We in Aglow can relate to Paul's desire to bond those young churches together in the faith. After 1967, when Aglow fellowships began bubbling up across the United States and in other countries, they needed encouragement. They needed to know the fullness of who they were in Christ. They needed relationship. Like Paul, our desire to reach out and nurture from far away birthed a series of Bible studies that have fed thousands since 1973 when our first study, *Genesis*, was published. Our studies share heart to heart, giving Christians new insights about themselves and their relationship with and in God.

In 1998, God's generous nature provided us a rewarding new relationship with Gospel Light. Together we published our Aglow classics as well as a selection of exciting new studies. Gospel Light began as a publishing ministry much in the same way Aglow began publishing Bible studies. Henrietta Mears formed Gospel Light in response to requests from churches across America for the Sunday School materials she had written. Gospel Light remains a strong ministry-minded witness for the gospel around the world.

Our heart's desire is that these studies will continue to kindle the minds of women and men, touch their hearts, and refresh their spirits with the light and life a loving Savior abundantly supplies.

This study, *A Woman After God's Heart* by Eadie Goodboy, will teach you what it means to be His daughter and experience the full adundant life that your heavenly Father intends for you in relationship to Him and His Body. I know its contents will richly reward you.

Jane Hansen-Hoyt
International President
Aglow International

INTRODUCTION

Paul's words "For to me, to live is Christ" (Philippians 1:21) were the living reality of his life. These words can and should be the heart cry of every Christian.

Christian women come in many different shapes, sizes, colors and backgrounds. Some of us sell real estate; others serve in restaurants or do accounting. Some of us carry briefcases or toolboxes; others carry diaper bags. But what we look like or what we do for a living really isn't that important. The important thing is that we love the Lord Jesus and desire to know Him better; that we serve Him faithfully and experience victory in the everyday routines of life.

The problem is that we often hurry from one task to another and get frustrated because we aren't *doing* more, and then we feel guilty because we're frustrated. We may read exciting books by Christians who have moved into what seems to be a new dimension in the Lord and wonder what's wrong with us. Futility sets in and with it comes a pattern of hopelessness.

But God has something better for us. He wants us to set aside our struggling and striving and allow Him to express Himself through us in an intensely personal way. Only as we yield to Him can we become His able ministers to a lost and dying world.

This study is designed to help you understand the practical aspects of the Christian walk and to nurture you in the process of attaining maturity. It is dedicated to you, a woman who has a personal relationship with Jesus and desires to grow into a mature person, walking victoriously with the Lord right where you are today. "With this in mind, we constantly pray for you, that our God may count you worthy of his calling, and that by his power he may fulfill every good purpose of yours and every act prompted by your faith. We pray this so that the name of our Lord Jesus may be glorified in you, and you in him, according to the grace of our God and the Lord Jesus Christ" (2 Thessalonians 1:11-12).

As we study and pray together, we trust the Holy Spirit will enlighten your understanding and renew your mind. Romans 12:2 in the *Amplified Version* says it well: "Be transformed (changed) by the [entire] renewal of your mind [by its new ideals and its new attitude], so that you may prove [for yourselves] what is the good and acceptable and perfect will of God, even the thing which is good and acceptable and perfect [in His sight for you]."

SPECIAL NOTE

The phrase "sons of God" in the New Testament includes both men and women. Passages such as John 1:12, which says that "as many as received him, to them gave he power to become the sons of God, even to them that believe on his name" (*KJV*), clearly does not limit salvation to the males of the species only, even though the Greek *huioi* is literally translated as "sons" in the *King James Version*. Almost all other translations, including the *New King James Version*, recognize the obvious inclusion of females and make the passage read "children of God." But even if we retain the *King James Version* rendition of "sons" in this verse, women need not be offended any more than men should be offended that God calls the Church the "bride of Christ." Just as men are not excluded from being part of the Bride of Christ, women are not excluded from being "sons of God" because they are women.

AN OVERVIEW OF THE STUDY

This Bible study is divided into four sections:

1. *A Closer Look at the Problem* defines the problem and the goal of the study.

2. *A Closer Look at God's Truth* gets you into God's Word. What does God have to say about what you are facing? How can you begin to apply His Word as you work through each lesson?

3. *A Closer Look at My Own Heart* will help you clarify and further apply biblical truths in your own life. It will also give guidance as you work toward becoming a woman after God's own heart.

4. *Action Steps I Can Take Today* is designed to help you focus on immediate steps of action.

WHAT YOU WILL NEED

· *A Bible*—The main Bible version used in this study is the *New International Version,* but you can use whatever Bible translation you are used to reading.

· *A Notebook*—During this study you will want to keep a journal to record what God shows you personally. You may also want to journal additional thoughts or feelings that come up as you go through the lessons. Some questions may require more space than is given in this study book.

· *Time to Meditate*—Only through meditation on what you're learning will you hear God's Word for you and begin to experience a heart knowledge, as well as a head knowledge, of the subject of being a woman after God's heart. Give the Holy Spirit time to personalize His Word to your heart so that you can know what your response should be to the knowledge you are gaining.

How to Start and Lead a Small Group

One key to leading a small group is to ask yourself, *What would Jesus do and how would He do it?* Jesus began His earthly ministry with a small group called the disciples, and the fact of His presence made wherever He was a safe place to be. Think of a small group as a safe place. It is a place that reflects God's heart and His hands. The way in which Jesus lived and worked with His disciples is a basic small-group model that we are able to draw both direction and nurture from.

Paul exhorted us to "walk in love, as Christ also has loved us and given Himself for us" (Ephesians 5:2, *NKJV*). We, as His earthly reflections, are privileged to walk in His footsteps, to help bind up the brokenhearted as He did or simply to listen with a compassionate heart. Whether you use this book as a Bible study, or as a focus point for a support group, a church group or a home group, walking in love means that we "bear one another's burdens" (Galatians 6:2, *NKJV*). The loving atmosphere provided by a small group can nourish, sustain and lift us up as nothing else can.

Jesus walked in love and spoke from an honest heart. In His endless well of compassion He never misplaced truth. Rather, He surrounded it with mercy. Those who left His presence felt good about themselves because Jesus used truth to point them in the right direction for their lives. When He spoke about the sinful woman who washed Jesus' feet with her tears and wiped them with her hair, He did not deny her sin. He said, "Her sins, which are many, are forgiven, for she loved much" (Luke 7:47, *NKJV*). That's honesty without condemnation.

Jesus was a model of servant leadership (see Mark 10:43-44). One of the key skills a group leader possesses is the ability to be an encourager of the group's members to grow spiritually. Keeping in personal contact with each member of the group, especially if one is absent, tells each one that he or she is important to the group. Other skills an effective group leader demonstrates include being a good listener, guiding the discussion, as well as guiding the group to deal with any conflicts that arise within it.

Whether you're a veteran or brand new to small-group leadership, virtually every group you lead will be different in personality and dynamic. The constant is the presence of Jesus Christ, and when He is at the group's center, everything else will come together.

OU'RE INVITED!

TO GROW . . .

To develop and reach maturity; thrive; to spring up;
come into existence from a source;

WITH A GROUP . . .

An assemblage of persons gathered or located together;
a number of individuals considered together because of similarities;

TO EXPLORE . . .

To investigate systematically; examine; search into or range over
for the purpose of discovery;

NEW TOPICS

Subject of discussion or conversation.

EETING

Date _____ Time _____

Place _____

_____

Contact _____

Phone _____

ONE

As a Fit Vessel

We hear people say, and have probably even said it ourselves, "I am attempting to live a good Christian life" or "I'm trying my best to serve the Lord." However, nowhere in the New Testament do the words "try" and "attempt" appear in the context of *doing* something for God. The reason is simple: The victorious Christian life is impossible to achieve by trying.

This chapter will help us begin to understand what it means to be "in Christ." It will also give practical insight into how we can daily yield ourselves to the Holy Spirit.

A Closer Look at the Problem

Think through your activities this past week, or even yesterday. How often did you trust in the Lord? How often did you act in your own strength?

On a scale of 1 to 10, rate how often you trusted in the Lord this past week—with 1 meaning *I didn't even think about God* and 10 meaning *I trusted totally in God and His power to do the work through me.* Explain why you gave yourself that rating.

_____

_____

_____

_____

_____

If you are like most people, the greater percentage of what you did was probably done in your own strength and abilities. God, however, wants us to know the reality of Paul's words, "When I am weak, then I am strong" (2 Corinthians 12:10) and "For to me, to live is Christ and to die is gain" (Philippians 1:21).

A Closer Look at God's Truth

LEARNING TO LET GO

Read Genesis 1:3,6,9,14; John 14:1; Philippians 2:5 (*KJV* or *NKJV*); and James 1:4 (*KJV* or *NKJV*). What is the key word in these verses that is the common denominator?

_____

_____

_____

_____

_____

This word holds the key to the victorious Christian experience. "Let" is synonymous with the words "allow" or "permit." *To allow* implies an absence of any attempt to hinder. *To permit* suggests assent or authorization. All three words simply mean that we are yielding ourselves—we are letting go of our wills and intellects and letting someone do something, or allowing something to happen by removing barriers or defenses.

This concept is one of flowing *with* God, even as His words "Let there be" flowed from Him in creation. We no longer pray to someone apart from us. We are "in Him." He lives in us and we flow together.

Read Jesus' prayer for His followers in John 17:20-23. What kind of relationship does Jesus want us to have with Himself and the Father?

_____

_____

_____

_____

_____

As we yield or flow with Him, what divine purpose is accomplished for the world to see?

_____

_____

_____

_____

_____

_____

What will be evident in our lives that will cause the world to know that the Father has indeed sent the Son?

_____

_____

_____

_____

_____

Read Romans 6:12-13. Write your definition of offering—yielding—yourself to God.

_____

_____

_____

_____

GOD'S THOUGHTS OR OUR THOUGHTS?

It is at the point of yielding where God meets resistance within us. Taught from childhood to believe that achievement entails struggle, we strive for good grades, parental favor, social acceptance and position. Then when we come to Jesus and His Word, we are confronted with commandments that contradict our natural way of thinking and acting. In the realm of spiritual laws, much that we have learned before knowing Christ must be relearned.

What does Paul admonish us to do in Romans 12:2?

_____

_____

_____

_____

This re-educating process takes place as one enters the school of the Spirit. Why, according to Isaiah 55:8, do we have difficulty in transforming our mindsets to God's mindset?

_____

_____

_____

_____

Give some examples of other scriptural principles that are opposed to our human reasoning (see Matthew 16:25; 20:26-27 to begin with).

_____

_____

_____

_____

YIELDED TO THE FATHER

When Jesus walked the earth, He was totally yielded to the Father. "For I have come down from heaven not to do my will but to do the will of him who sent me" (John 6:38). In complete yieldedness, Jesus broke the power of sin and death when He took the punishment for our sin on the cross.

Although Jesus' redemption work was finished at Calvary, there is still much to be done on earth. According to Matthew 28:19-20; John 14:12 and Acts 1:8, who is to continue on with the work of Jesus?

_____

_____

_____

_____

Read Galatians 2:20; Philippians 4:13 and Colossians 1:26-27. Again we ask, who is to finish the work?

_____

_____

_____

_____

YIELDING TO THE SON

But how do we finish God's work? In Philippians 1:21, Paul wrote, "For to me, to live is Christ." But what does that mean?

Jesus is present today on earth in His Body, the Church, of which every believer is a part. God's purpose is to express Himself through us as He did with Jesus when He was on earth. God's Word, especially the New Testament, provides a pattern for us to follow.

As His adopted daughters, we are to learn from the only begotten Son. He teaches us that we are to be clean channels through which His love and the power of His Holy Spirit can flow (see Romans 6:13; 12:1-2; 1 Peter

2:11-12). But we can only do that as we yield to Him and let Him minister through us to a love-starved world.

If our lives become clogged with unconfessed sin, we limit His power, for He works through us in proportion to our counting ourselves dead to sin and alive to God in Christ Jesus (see Romans 6:11). However, we may know this fact and still experience defeat and discouragement. It is possible to intellectually grasp the concept of "Christ in me" without allowing the knowledge to pass into actual experience. Why? Because it involves discipline.

Read Ephesians 6:11-13. To what occupation does Paul compare our Christian lives?

_____

_____

_____

_____

What kind of discipline is necessary in this occupation?

_____

_____

_____

_____

Why is it particularly necessary to be disciplined in our minds (verse 11)?

_____

_____

_____

_____

Read 2 Corinthians 10:5 and complete the sentence: "We take _____ every _____ to make it _____ to Christ." Our victory has been given us by grace, but the discipline is a necessary part of our development as servants of the Lord.

A Closer Look at My Own Heart

As you begin to discipline and renew your mind to a consciousness of Christ's indwelling presence, you will become aware of Him in every situation. Your daily life will take on a new vitality, a sense of expectation and adventure. You can make Paul's declaration, "For to me, to live is Christ" (Philippians 1:21), your very own.

In moments of temptation and frustration you can learn to say, "Holy Spirit, I yield to You." When you say and mean that, something happens.

An example: Dinner is ready. Your husband comes home hot and ruffled from a busy day at the office. The mail has been misplaced, your two-year-old rushes to welcome Daddy, stumbles and bruises his lip. The dog barks and the rice begins to burn. When you remember to pray, "Holy Spirit, I yield to You," a quietness returns within your spirit and you receive the blessing: "Now may the Lord of peace Himself grant you His peace (the peace of His kingdom) at all times and in all ways [under all circumstances and conditions, whatever comes]" (2 Thessalonians 3:16, *AMP*).

Consider a situation in your own life similar to the one mentioned in the preceding paragraph where you were able to say (or should have said), "Holy Spirit, I yield to You." What occurred as a result of your yieldedness (or lack of yieldedness)?

_____

_____

_____

_____

Warning: Yielding to the Holy Spirit may require a change of attitude, conversation or activity!

Action Steps I Can Take Today

Write Philippians 1:21, Galatians 2:20 and 2 Thessalonians 3:16 on one side of a 3x5-inch card. On the other side write, "Holy Spirit, I yield to You." Make a commitment to read these verses each morning this week, and then take the card with you through your day. Ask God to remind you to pray your prayer of surrender whenever you are faced with a temptation or frustration.

Consider asking a friend, preferably someone also going through this study, to be your prayer partner. Ask your prayer partner to pray for you and keep you accountable as you work through this study. Share with your prayer partner what happens in your life this week as a result of praying the yielding prayer when you faced a difficult situation.

TWO

IN THE SPIRIT AND IN THE WORD

PART ONE: IN THE SPIRIT

As we begin to be aware of the constant indwelling presence of Jesus through consciously yielding to Him, we become more sensitive to the Holy Spirit's leading. Freedom from self—yieldedness to God—produces His joy in us. When our rebellious and selfish attitudes assert themselves, we experience grief. We are like clay pots being lovingly molded and reworked by our Father into vessels useful for His service (see Isaiah 64:8).

A Closer Look at the Problem

Being a vessel in the hands of the Master does not mean, however, that we will not have problems. As long as we are on earth, there will be times when we will experience testings or temptations. Consciousness of the Lord's presence may even fade for a while.

The goal of this chapter is to equip us with an understanding of God's work during these times. "For who has known or understood the mind (the counsels and purposes) of the Lord so as to guide and instruct Him and give Him knowledge? But we have the mind of Christ (the Messiah) and do hold the thoughts (feelings and purposes) of His heart" (1 Corinthians 2:16, *AMP*).

A Closer Look at God's Truth

Read Luke 3:21-22. When everyone else had been baptized, Jesus was also baptized. What happened as He was praying and probably still standing in the water?

_____

_____

_____

Many Christians believe that this event corresponds to what is known to-day as the baptism of the Holy Spirit. What do you think?

_____

_____

_____

_____

_____

According to Luke 4:1-2, after Jesus was baptized, He was led by the Spirit into the desert. For what purpose did the Spirit lead Him there (also see Matthew 4:1)?

_____

_____

_____

_____

_____

Read Luke 4:14-16. After returning from the desert experiences, how was Jesus described (verse 14)?

_____

_____

_____

_____

The power of the Holy Spirit was upon Jesus as He came out of the desert. He went into this experience of wilderness temptation led by the Spirit. He came out of it in the power of the Spirit. The same should be true in our lives. When we go into any experience of testing or temptation, we should acknowledge the Spirit's leading. When we come out of it, we should experience His power.

Explain how you have found this presence of God's power after a time of testing to be evident in your life or in the lives of others.

_____

_____

_____

_____

_____

Read Romans 8:28-29. Why are testings and problems allowed in the lives of Christians?

_____

_____

_____

_____

What is the Father's purpose for allowing them (verse 29)? Also read 1 Peter 1:6-7.

_____

_____

_____

_____

According to James 1:2-4, what virtue is the Holy Spirit endeavoring to bring to fruition in our Christian walk?

_____

_____

_____

_____

A GLIMPSE OF THE FUTURE

According to 2 Timothy 2:12a; Revelation 3:21 and 22:3-5, what future role is the Father preparing for His children?

_____

_____

_____

_____

Earthly kings submit their heirs to highly disciplined, rigorous training to prepare them for their responsibilities as rulers. How much more must the King of kings lovingly but firmly train and equip His children for future co-leadership with Christ who is over all things.

THE CALL TO CONTINUE

Even though we are being trained for leadership in Christ's heavenly kingdom, we have to realize that, just as we did not enter kindergarten and graduate from high school in the same year, neither can we expect to graduate from the school of the Spirit in a few weeks or months. Just as it takes time for fruit to mature, it takes time for God's Word to grow to maturity in our lives.

Compare the phrase "Perseverance [patience] must finish its work" (James 1:4) with Philippians 3:12-14: "Not that I have now attained [this ideal], or have already been made perfect, but I press on to lay hold of (grasp) and make my own, that for which Christ Jesus (the Messiah) has laid hold of me and made me His own. I do not consider, brethren, that I have captured and made it my own [yet]; but one thing I do [it is my one aspiration]: forgetting what lies behind and straining forward to what lies ahead, I press on toward the goal to win the [supreme and heavenly] prize to which God in Christ Jesus is calling us upward" (*AMP*).

_____

_____

_____

_____

What further insights do you learn from your Teacher?

_____

_____

_____

_____

LIGHT IN DARK PLACES

The Holy Spirit is a compassionate teacher. As we yield to His control, He leads us gently along, but we have a choice. As He sheds light on our dark areas, we may either choose to yield to Him and continue to grow in Christlikeness, or choose not to yield. The choice is always ours. However, the Lord cannot take us further until these hindrances have been dealt with.

According to 1 John 1:9, what does God promise us when we confess our sins to Him?

_____

_____

_____

_____

According to Colossians 1:9-12, how does God want us to live our lives now?

_____

_____

_____

_____

What inner source gives us the ability to live such a life (also see Ephesians 1:17-20)?

_____

_____

_____

_____

How are you going to utilize this power?

_____

_____

_____

_____

GROWING THROUGH HARD PLACES
We often come to hard places in our Christian walk when our weaknesses threaten to overwhelm us and we are tempted to give up.

Read 2 Corinthians 12:9-10 and Philippians 4:13. What encouragement is in these verses?

_____

_____

_____

_____

It is only as we allow the Spirit to reveal our weaknesses that we are able to submit to the power of the indwelling Lord. According to Luke 22:41-44 and Hebrews 5:7-8, what quality of Sonship did Jesus learn through His sufferings and trials?

_____

_____

_____

_____

A Closer Look at My Own Heart

Those in the family of God are learning obedience—sometimes as an experience of joy, sometimes through suffering. But we do not have to wait until we are with the Lord to realize all the results of our maturing; we can begin to see them here on earth.

> And after you have suffered a little while, the God of all grace [Who imparts all blessing and favor], Who has called you to His [own] eternal glory in Christ Jesus, will Himself complete and make you what you ought to be, establish and ground you securely, and strengthen, and settle you (1 Peter 5:10, *AMP*).

According to Isaiah 1:19 and Micah 6:8, what qualities does the Lord require of you, His daughter?

_____

_____

_____

_____

Evaluate your spiritual maturity while reading and meditating on Galatians 5:22-23 and 2 Peter 1:5-8. List the character traits/qualities produced by the Holy Spirit when we live a life of obedience.

_____

_____

_____

_____

Choose one of the above traits that you feel is most lacking in your life right now and make an acrostic by writing the letters of the word vertically down a piece of paper. Add words and/or phrases horizontally to describe that quality. For example:

Press on and
Allow His Spirit full control when
Trials test me.
I will wait upon the Lord,
Endure and
Not get ahead of God's plan.
Crises will come, but God will
Enable me to handle them.

Action Steps I Can Take Today

Ask a friend/your prayer partner to pray specifically for you to develop the spiritual fruit that you chose in the previous activity. Spend some time sharing and planning together about how you might begin to cultivate this character quality. Be sure to remind one another that you can grow in this area only as you allow the Holy Spirit to do the work. Your responsibility is to yield to Him and obey His instructions.

_____

_____

_____

_____

At the end of the week, ask yourself, *How is the Holy Spirit dealing with me on this particular aspect of my spiritual development?* Write down what you believe He is teaching you so that it is clear in your thinking.

_____

_____

_____

_____

PART TWO: IN THE WORD

A popular saying states, "The only things certain in this world are death and taxes." But this is not true. According to Isaiah 40:8, the Word of God is certain and it will stand forever.

Over the centuries men have repeatedly tried to destroy God's Word, but He has always preserved it, even through extremely perilous times. It is important that we know that the Bible is living and powerful and as relevant to our lives today as when it was first given (see Hebrews 4:12).

This chapter will help us understand how we can submit to the Holy Spirit and allow God's Word to renew and change us.

A Closer Look at the Problem

Just as we require daily food to nourish our physical bodies, so too do we require spiritual food for the nurturing of our renewed minds. One evidence of rebirth is a hunger for the Word of God: the desire to know God, to understand and obey His commandments, to seek out and claim His promises. The Bible is our textbook in the school of the Spirit.

Describe how a textbook is used by a student who is enrolled in a course of study.

_____

_____

_____

_____

_____

A Closer Look at God's Truth

GOD'S WORD IS ALIVE

Read John 1:1-3,14. Who is being referred to as God's Word?

_____

_____

_____

_____

_____

According to these verses, what did the Word do?

_____

_____

_____

_____

When we love Jesus, we love the Word, because He is the Word. When we read and meditate on Scripture, we are making God's written truth a part of ourselves. Jesus is not the Bible, which is also referred to as the Word, but He is God's living expression of truth.

According to Deuteronomy 8:3, of what importance was the Word of God to the children of Israel?

_____

_____

_____

_____

Read Exodus 16:4-36 and John 6:48-58. Explain in your own words how the life-giving manna was like Christ.

_____

_____

_____

_____

_____

Compare the similarities and differences between the eating of manna and feeding on the Bread of Life.

_____

_____

_____

_____

_____

Read Luke 4:1-12. Of what importance was the Word of God to Jesus?

_____

_____

_____

_____

_____

Just as the devil knew the written Word and how to use it for his own purposes, so too it is possible for a person to read the Word of God and never come to know Jesus as Savior. There is only One who can reveal life-giving truth; He reveals it to the person who seeks Him (see Luke 11:9-10). This is the reason we humbly ask the Holy Spirit to teach us as we read God's Word.

GOD'S WORD CAN BE TRUSTED
Read Numbers 23:19 and 2 Timothy 2:13. Why is it safe to trust in God and His Word?

_____

_____

_____

_____

_____

We are a part of Him and He cannot disown Himself. Unlike us, God is without moods or whims. He is forever fixed in His character—in this instance, His faithfulness.

_____

_____

_____

_____

GOD'S WORD CAN BE UNDERSTOOD
Read John 6:45-65. From the context of this passage, what did Jesus mean when He said, "The words I have spoken to you are spirit and they are life" (verse 63)?

_____

_____

_____

_____

After Jesus' death and resurrection, He was seen during the next forty days by various groups before He finally ascended to the Father. On one occasion the resurrected Lord ate with the disciples and "then He [thoroughly] opened up their minds to understand the Scriptures" (Luke 24:45, *AMP*). What eagerness to understand His teaching must have filled their hearts that day. Jesus continues to teach believers today through the Scriptures and the revelation of the Holy Spirit.

GOD'S WORD HELPS US GROW SPIRITUALLY
According to 2 Timothy 3:16-17, how does Scripture help us grow into spiritual maturity?

_____

_____

_____

From the day a baby is born, he begins to grow and develop. He wiggles, rolls, crawls and, finally, after several stumbling attempts, begins to walk. Speech develops as each new word takes on meaning. So it is with a new Christian. God's Word is a lamp to our feet and a light for our paths (see Psalm 119:105). How gently the Holy Spirit illumines our walk with Him. How tenderly He leads us to know and do His will.

Read Hebrews 5:13–6:1 and 1 Peter 2:2. Using these verses as a basis, explain what you think is the difference between "milk" and "solid food."

_____

_____

_____

_____

Both the new birth and the baptism in the Holy Spirit are foundational experiences. Through them we step from one dimension of spiritual awareness into another. But we must keep on stepping. Second Timothy 2:15 tells us:

> Study and be eager and do your utmost to present yourself to God approved (tested by trial), a workman who has no cause to be ashamed, correctly analyzing and accurately dividing [rightly handling and skillfully teaching] the Word of Truth (*AMP*).

We are to make God's approval our goal. As daughters of God we should have an eagerness, motivated by the Holy Spirit, to do our utmost, so that we can stand before the Father unashamed in our correct knowledge of Him—the Word of Truth, the Lord Jesus. Irving L. Jensen puts it like this: "The real test of the heart's relation to God is obedience to His Word."

Read 1 Corinthians 2:12 and 2 Timothy 3:17. For what purpose has Scripture and the Spirit been given?

_____

_____

_____

_____

According to the following verses, what will the Word of God produce in our lives?

Psalm 107:20

_____

_____

_____

_____

Romans 10:17

_____

_____

_____

_____

Hebrews 5:14

_____

_____

_____

_____

1 Peter 1:23

_____

_____

_____

_____

List the particular attitudes we should have concerning the Word of God found in Psalm 119:11-18.

_____

_____

_____

_____

Compare your attitudes toward the Word with David's in Psalm 119. Which attitudes are the same?

_____

_____

_____

_____

Which attitudes are lacking in your heart?

_____

_____

_____

_____

What are some other effects produced by the Word in our lives?

Psalm 119:105

_____
_____
_____

Acts 20:32

_____
_____
_____

Hebrews 4:12

_____
_____
_____

In Paul's explanation of the Christian's spiritual armor in Ephesians 6:11-17, he has instructed us to take up the "sword of the Spirit, which is the word of God" (verse 17). It is significant that it is the only piece of the armor that is used as an offensive weapon. If it is used skillfully and correctly (see Hebrews 4:12) in witnessing, what will the sword of the Spirit accomplish in the lives of unbelievers?

_____
_____
_____
_____

A Closer Look at My Own Heart

In Psalm 119:11, David states, "I have hidden your word in my heart that I might not sin against you." What do you think David meant by this statement?

_____
_____
_____
_____

How could you apply these words to your own heart?

_____

_____

_____

_____

Action Steps I Can Take Today

Choose the verse from this lesson that has been the most meaningful to you. Hide it in your heart by memorizing it. Ask the Lord to show you someone who needs your verse and share it with him or her!

The following verse is stated as a command. It is for NOW—TODAY—and is as up-to-date as today's newspaper:

> And these words which I am commanding you this day shall be [first] in your own mind and heart; [then] you shall whet and sharpen them so as to make them penetrate, and teach and impress them diligently upon the [minds and] hearts of your children, and shall talk of them when you sit in your house, and when you walk by the way, and when you lie down and when you rise up (Deuteronomy 6:6-7, *AMP*).

What are some ways in which you can begin to incorporate the Word into practical daily living in your home? List them, then ask the Holy Spirit to show you which one He wants you to implement this week. Ask your prayer partner to pray for you as you commit yourself to obediently living out what He has revealed to you.

As we think about the power we have available through the penetrating truth of the Word and prayer focused on the bringing down of strongholds, let us remember daily the one billion Muslim and Chinese women who struggle in darkness, that they might also become God's daughters. Pray for these oppressed women on a regular basis.

THREE

MINISTERING PRAISE

For the LORD will rebuild Zion and appear in his glory. He will respond to the prayer of the destitute; he will not despise their plea. Let this be written for a future generation, that a people not yet created may praise the LORD.

PSALM 102:16-18

In these verses David prophesied the triumphal second coming of Jesus after He has rebuilt Zion (Jerusalem). We are blessed to be living in the time of Israel's national restoration, the final ingathering that is to precede and make Zion ready for His coming.

At this time, Christians are experiencing reunification in the Body of Christ; the Holy Spirit is calling His people to be a great family of lovers— lovers of Jesus and of one another. This chapter will draw our hearts nearer to God and to one another in worship and praise.

A Closer Look at the Problem

Sometimes it's hard to praise the Lord. Which of the following have you experienced recently?

- ❏ The temperature is over 101 degrees three days in a row and you have no air-conditioning.
- ❏ Your out-of-town visitors stay an extra week.
- ❏ Your dog vomits on the rug.
- ❏ You can't get home for the holidays because the airlines have shut down.

In spite of our feelings or our circumstances, God's Word is clear. We are commanded to worship the Lord and sing praises to His holy name even when circumstances are not to our liking. His Word gives us insight into how we are to praise and worship Him, no matter the circumstances.

A Closer Look at God's Truth

Choosing to Worship

When we think of praise, we often think of David. Though he sinned greatly in God's sight, he was quick to acknowledge his sin, repent and return to fellowship. He was a man after God's own heart (see Acts 13:22; see also 1 Samuel 13:14). Psalm 22:3 tells us that God is enthroned upon the praises of His people. When we worship Him we can know with certainty that He is there.

Read Deuteronomy 10:21; 1 Chronicles 16:34; 1 Peter 1:3; 2:9 and Revelation 5:12-14. What reasons are given for worshiping God?

_____

_____

_____

_____

_____

There may be times when we are burdened with griefs and cares and are not conscious of the Lord's presence. But as soon as we seek the Lord Jesus, we begin to worship. A change occurs in our perspective as we focus on Him. As we meditate on His attributes and begin to praise Him, our faith increases. So does our expectancy; we can thank and praise Him for an answer to the problem (see Matthew 21:22). Praise releases God to work. Praise releases us to believe.

Read Psalm 57:6-7; 108:1. Despite the distressing situation of his life, what was David's attitude?

_____

_____

_____

_____

_____

The Whats, Wheres, Whens, Hows and Whys of Praise

Praise is a constant and conscious attitude, a way of thinking that is positive and spiritually healthy. As the Holy Spirit works in our spirits, freeing us from inhibitions and traditional formalities, we begin to grow in a new dimension of praise.

According to 1 Peter 2:9, what are four reasons we should praise God?

_____

_____

_____

_____

Where is it acceptable to praise the Lord according to the following passages?

Psalm 111:1

_____

_____

_____

_____

Psalm 149:5

_____

_____

_____

_____

Psalm 150:1

_____

_____

_____

_____

Acts 16:25

_____

_____

_____

_____

Ephesians 5:19

_____

_____

_____

_____

When is it acceptable to praise the Lord according to the following?

Psalm 34:1

_____

_____

_____

_____

Psalm 57:8

_____

_____

_____

Psalm 119:62

_____

_____

_____

How is it acceptable to praise the Lord?

Psalm 47:1,6-7

_____

_____

_____

Psalm 109:30

_____

_____

_____

Psalm 119:7

_____

_____

_____

Psalm 138:1

_____
_____
_____
_____
_____

Psalm 150:3-5

_____
_____
_____
_____

Why do we praise the Lord?

Revelation 4:11

_____
_____
_____
_____

Revelation 5:12

_____
_____
_____
_____

SINGING, DANCING AND LIFTING OUR HANDS

The Hebrew people praised the Lord with cornets, trumpets, flutes, pipes, cymbals and stringed instruments. "Let them praise His name in chorus and choir and with the [single or group] dance" (Psalm 149:3, *AMP*). We may sing and dance before the Lord as an act of worship; it is pleasing to Him.

As Christian women who belong to the generation of praise, we probably understand that it is also pleasing to the Father when we lift our hands to Him. Read the following verses and see if you can discover in each one a particular attitude or reason for uplifted hands.

Psalm 28:2

_____

_____

_____

_____

Psalm 63:2-4

_____

_____

_____

_____

Psalm 134:1-2

_____

_____

_____

_____

Psalm 143:6

_____

_____

_____

_____

1 Timothy 2:8

_____

_____

_____

_____

Our goal is to glorify Him in everything we do, including the manner in which we praise Him. If scriptural principles are adhered to, we can know that we are walking in truth and are pleasing our Lord.

THE SACRIFICE OF PRAISE
In addition to these kinds of praise, Scripture gives enlightenment on a different concept: the sacrifice of praise. Read the following Scripture passages and answer the questions.

Psalm 119:108. What sacrifice is David referring to here?

_____

_____

_____

_____

Hebrews 13:15. Why do you think the word "sacrifice" is used in conjunction with praising?

_____

_____

_____

_____

Jonah 2:1-10. In Jonah's case, what was the result of his sacrifice of praise?

_____

_____

_____

_____

The Word of God teaches us that God delights in our praises. How much more must be His delight as we choose to praise Him when to do so is a sacrifice. This sacrifice of praise is an expression of deep trust; it brings us near to God and brings pleasure to His heart.

A Closer Look at My Own Heart

When we received Jesus as Savior, we stepped into a relationship that had all the potential of vitality and intimacy. From then on, we should be living for His purposes, not our own.

According to Ephesians 1:12, what is His purpose for each believer?

_____

_____

_____

_____

Do you realize that your purpose and destiny is to cause His glory to be praised? Since God is a Spirit, He cannot be perceived through the senses.

But people can recognize Him by His characteristics. They behold Him in Jesus.

Since Jesus' ascension, others recognize Jesus' characteristics in His people. This only happens as each one of us allows God to be magnified in us personally. Only then can people praise Him for what they see. As Christian women, we will never be fulfilled until we become that for which we were created: women who are the praise of His glory!

> The Lord your God is in the midst of you, a Mighty One, a Savior [Who saves]! He will rejoice over you with joy; He will rest [in silent satisfaction] and in His love He will be silent and make no mention [of past sins, or even recall them]; He will exult over you with singing (Zephaniah 3:17, *AMP*).

This is the assurance that you, as God's daughter, can hang on to in troubling times. Your Father is *always* present. He rejoices in exultation because of you. Ask God to stir in you a desire to live completely for Him, thanking and praising Him for all that He is.

Action Steps I Can Take Today

Gratitude and joy are part of our praise. "Always be joyful. Always keep on praying. No matter what happens, always be thankful, for this is God's will for you who belong to Christ Jesus" (1 Thessalonians 5:16-18, *TLB*).

Name eight things for which you can praise the Lord today. Be specific—recent answers to prayer, witnessing, healing, etc. Also list those things for which you are trusting Him as you praise—unsaved loved ones, marriage problems, finances, and so forth.

What is one particular difficult circumstance in your life today for which you can offer the sacrifice of praise? After you have written it down, mark on your calendar when this Bible study ends. On that day plan to record how the situation has changed or how you have been changed in the situation. Until that date, choose to make the sacrifice of praise at least once daily.

How does it make you feel to realize that you are part of that future generation Psalm 102:18 talks about?

Write Ephesians 5:19-20 on a 3 x 5-inch card and carry it with you. Read it often throughout the day. It will put a song in your heart—a song that you can pass on to those who cross your path during the day!

FOUR

MINISTERING SERVICE AND HOSPITALITY

PART ONE: MINISTERING SERVICE

In the last chapter we learned how much the praises of our lips delight our heavenly Father. In this lesson we will discover how we can serve Him in practical ways: our lips, our hands, our feet and our bodies dedicated to His service. Our goal is that we may say with David, "I desire to do your will, O my God" (Psalm 40:8).

A Closer Look at the Problem

Have you ever wished you had lived in the days when Jesus physically walked the earth? Would you have enjoyed the opportunity of opening your home to Him as Mary and Martha did, or anointing His feet with your perfume? Would you have delighted in mending and washing His garments?

When you think of the phrase "serving the Lord," what comes to mind?

_____

_____

_____

_____

Picture how you might have spent a day with Jesus when He was on earth. What personal act of service would you have particularly enjoyed doing for Him?

_____

_____

_____

_____

Is service to God a continual thing or is it an action we perform at appointed times? Explain your answer.

_____

_____

_____

_____

A Closer Look at God's Truth

JESUS, THE PERFECT SERVANT

Each of us has a distinctive place of service in the kingdom of God and Jesus is our supreme example of a perfect servant. He lived to serve the Father and His followers.

What can we learn about servanthood from Jesus' words and actions? Read the following verses and answer the questions:

Luke 22:27. What did Jesus say about Himself?

_____

_____

_____

John 13:12-17. Describe what Jesus had done and the attitude in which He had done it.

_____

_____

_____

Mark 10:45. What was Jesus' greatest and final earthly act of service?

_____

_____

_____

Isaiah 52:13 and Philippians 2:6-11—Name *one* of the results of Jesus' service to the Father.

_____

_____

_____

FOLLOWING THE MASTER

What kinds of acceptable services are described in the following verses?

Luke 2:36-37

_____

_____

_____

Romans 1:9

_____

_____

_____

2 Timothy 1:3

_____

_____

_____

As we enter into service for our Father, what kinds of heart attitudes does He desire that we have?

Psalm 2:11

_____

_____

_____

_____

Psalm 100:2

_____

_____

_____

_____

Acts 20:19

_____

_____

_____

Colossians 3:23

_____

_____

_____

According to Colossians 3:24, why does God want us to have these attitudes?

_____

_____

_____

_____

Paul considered himself a servant of Christ. In his letters, he often encouraged his readers to cultivate a servant heart. Look up the following verses and respond to the questions.

2 Timothy 2:24-26. Describe other important qualities of a servant.

_____

_____

_____

Galatians 5:13. How then are we to serve?

_____

_____

_____

We joyfully serve one whom we love. Jesus Christ, living in us and through us, loves those we serve.

LEARNING FROM THE MASTER

Read John 13:1-17. This passage often describes the great servant-heart of our Lord. As you read it, pay special attention to verse 3. Write down three important facts that Jesus knew about Himself before He began to wash the disciples' feet.

_____

_____

_____

_____

_____

Would knowing what He knew regarding His power, His source and His future have made it easier or more difficult for Him to perform such a menial task? Why?

_____

_____

_____

_____

Jesus, with perfect assurance and confidence, was free to love and graciously serve to the utmost. We, as His adopted children and coheirs, are called to follow His example. According to Ephesians 1:3-5,18-19 and John 14:2, what are we promised because of our relationship with Him?

_____

_____

_____

Compare what Jesus knew about Himself and what we know about ourselves in the above verses. How are we similar?

_____

_____

_____

_____

A Closer Look at My Own Heart

SERVING WITH THE MASTER

God's Word gives us such confidence that we, as true daughters of our God and Father, are as free and secure as Jesus was to joyfully and humbly perform lowly tasks.

The more we yield to the Spirit, the more love we have for the Father and the more our love and service grows. He is loving others through us; we are seeing them through His eyes. Although He is ministering, He is using our yielded personalities, our wills and our bodies. In every incident of yieldedness, we are conforming just a little more to His image (see 2 Corinthians 3:18).

What was Jesus trying to teach His disciples in John 12:23-26?

_____

_____

_____

_____

Just as Jesus yielded His life for us, so too are we called to yield our lives to Him and follow Him to serve where He would serve. Jesus is everywhere there is a need: a sick friend, a new Christian who needs counseling and encouragement, our own children, unsaved loved ones, a wounded animal—the list is endless. Jesus is there and He is calling us to be there too. His people working together can meet the needs of mankind as He ministers through His children.

Read John 12:26 again. As we flow together in Christ and He is in us ministering to others, what will the Father do?

_____

_____

_____

_____

Our Lord is gracious. Not only did He give entirely of Himself at Calvary, but He has also promised that the Father will honor us as we serve Him. Our short years on earth are to be lived as preparation time for what the Lord has waiting for us in heaven.

Read Revelation 22:3. What else besides praising and rejoicing will we be doing in heaven?

_____

_____

_____

How can you prepare yourself now so that you will be ready to serve your heavenly Father in eternity?

_____

_____

_____

Action Steps I Can Take Today

When Jesus Christ called you to be His daughter, He also called you to make Him Lord of your life. You cannot serve two masters—you either serve sin or you serve God (see Matthew 6:24).

Jesus will never force His lordship on you. Nor will He burden you with impossible tasks. He is your gentle Shepherd, and as you learn to follow Him you will grow in your appreciation of who He is and what He wants to do in and through your life.

Look back over this section and meditate on the truths you have studied. Prayerfully ask Him how He would desire you to express your love for Him and others this week; then complete the following sentences:

Lord Jesus, I want to demonstrate my love for You personally today by . . .

I know now that one of the ways I can serve You best is by serving others. One person who comes into my mind right now is _____. One way I can serve her/him this week is by . . .

PART TWO: MINISTERING HOSPITALITY

In part one of this chapter, we examined what it meant to serve the Lord. We also learned that our service here on earth is one way we prepare to serve Him in heaven. In part two, we will focus more closely on the practical aspects of serving Him in our homes.

A Closer Look at the Problem

One of the highest privileges we have as Christian women is to practice hospitality. Women have been created by God to nurture others, and creating a home of welcome and warmth can be a part of this nurturing.

In this second half of this chapter, we will discover how our homes can become places set apart for Him. Whether we live in a large home or a small apartment, we all live somewhere; that "somewhere" is the special spot in which God has placed each of us. As we yield to Him, our homes become sanctified places—set apart, consecrated to the Lord. Wherever a Christian dwells, there dwells the presence of the Holy Spirit.

Look around the place where you dwell. What do you see in your home as an obstacle to practicing hospitality?

_____

_____

_____ .

What about your own attitude? What ways of thinking and doing things have you developed that might be keeping you from serving God in this way?

_____

_____

_____

Even though our homes may not be all that we desire them to be, we can be assured that God wants us to use them to minister to others. Women in particular have been given the blessing of opening their homes to God's people. The Scriptures in this section give outstanding examples of hospitality and its rewards and blessings.

A Closer Look at God's Truth

Read 1 Kings 17:7-24. What was the attitude of this widow toward Elijah and toward the Lord?

_____

_____

_____

_____

As a result of her attitude, what rewards did she receive?

_____

_____

_____

Read 2 Kings 4:8-37. What are the differences in the circumstances surrounding the home of the widow of Zarephath and the Shunammite woman?

_____

_____

_____

_____

What blessings did this woman receive as a result of her hospitality to a servant of God?

_____

_____

_____

_____

RAHAB'S HOSPITALITY

The hospitality of Rahab, the harlot, toward the Israelite spies is recorded in Joshua. Risking death and danger to herself and her family, Rahab protected the two spies and helped them escape from Jericho.

Read Joshua 2:1-23. In what way was she rewarded for this ministry to them (see Joshua 6:20-25)?

_____

_____

_____

_____

Read Hebrews 11:31 and James 2:25. For what two virtues is this woman remembered in the New Testament?

_____

_____

_____

_____

Rahab was a heathen woman, yet as she grew in her understanding of God and His purpose for the children of Israel, she risked all to serve Him. God bestowed on her the honor of becoming the great-great-grandmother of King David and, therefore, a member of the godly line from which came Jesus Christ, the Messiah (see Matthew 1:5).

It is the same today, for the ways of the Father never change. As we give, it is given back to us. As we open our homes in sincere hospitality, those to whom we minister will bring blessing to us.

ABRAHAM'S HOSPITALITY

Read Genesis 18. List what Abraham did for his three guests in the following verses:

Genesis 18:2

_____

_____

_____

Genesis 18:4

_____

_____

_____

Genesis 18:5

_____

_____

_____

Genesis 18:6

_____

_____

_____

Genesis 18:7

_____

_____

_____

Genesis 18:8

_____

_____

_____

Underline the verbs in the above list of Abraham's actions. Do you think that Abraham guessed who was coming to dinner? Explain your answer.

_____

_____

_____

_____

_____

What was Abraham's attitude as a host?

_____

_____

_____

_____

_____

What blessing does the Lord offer Abraham in verse 14?

_____

_____

_____

_____

One of the results of Abraham's diligence in hospitality is recorded in verse 32 when God promised to spare his nephew Lot and his family from the destruction of Sodom and Gomorrah.

PRACTICING HOSPITALITY

As you read the following verses, list the people to whom God wants us to practice hospitality.

Isaiah 58:7

_____

_____

_____

_____

Luke 14:13

_____

_____

_____

_____

Romans 12:13

_____

_____

_____

_____

Romans 12:20

_____

_____

_____

Hebrews 13:2

_____

_____

_____

Why should we be diligent to practice hospitality toward the people who come to our homes?

_____

_____

_____

_____

SHARING JESUS

There are countless ways in which we can share Jesus: over a cup of coffee with a neighbor or a dinner with all the trimmings for a coworker, a chip-and-dip talk session with teenagers, or a cup of tea with a home Bible study group. We may share Christ by opening our homes to unbelievers as well as believers. As we do, we must remember that the attitude by which we practice the ministry of hospitality is of utmost importance.

What were the children of Israel commanded to do in Deuteronomy 10:19?

_____

_____

_____

The dictionary defines "hospitality" as "the reception and entertainment of guests or strangers with generosity and kindness." On a scale of 1 to 10 (with 1 being poor and 10 being excellent), how would you rate your home in the ministry of hospitality?

_____

_____

_____

A Closer Look at My Own Heart

One of the ways you can grow in the area of hospitality is to ask God to help you begin to see each person He brings into your home through the eyes of Jesus. As you yield to Him, He will be able to care for their needs through you.

This includes strangers as well as friends, the unsaved as well as your Christian brothers and sisters. Jesus said, "In so far as you did it for one of the least [in the estimation of men] of these My brethren, you did it for Me" (Matthew 25:40, *AMP*).

Since our homes reflect ourselves and our Lord, keeping them tidy and clean should be a priority. This does not mean that our homes look like the model homes in decorating magazines, but it does mean that we learn to put first things first. Making your home a welcoming place does require effort. Household chores take on a new meaning when we begin to do them "as to the Lord." Even dirty corners can become a joy when we scrub them for Him and His glory.

Action Steps I Can Take Today

Write the following verse on a 3 x 5-inch card: "Practice hospitality to one another (those of the household of faith). [Be hospitable, be a lover of strangers, with brotherly affection for the unknown guests, the foreigners, the poor, and all others who come your way who are of Christ's body.] And [in each instance] do it ungrudgingly (cordially and graciously, without complaining but as representing Him)" (1 Peter 4:9, *AMP*).

On the other side of the card write down two things you could do that will improve your home and make it more usable in the ministry of hospitality.

Has the Lord been nudging your mind about opening your home for a Bible study or having a couple over for dinner so that you might share the love of Christ? What can you do this week to begin practicing hospitality?

Ask your prayer partner to keep you accountable to carry through on this plan.

FIVE

MANAGING THE FATHER'S AFFAIRS

When we belong to God, all we have belongs to Him, too. As a token, we are to lay aside a percentage of our income for the Lord. This principle, known as tithing, is first recorded in Genesis 14:18-20 when Abram offered one tenth of his possessions to the high priest, Melchizedek. Mosaic law instituted tithing in Leviticus 27:30-33 and Numbers 18:25-26. In Malachi 3:10 we are instructed:

> Bring all the tithes (the whole tenth of your income) into the storehouse, that there may be food in My house, and prove Me now by it, says the Lord of hosts, if I will not open the windows of heaven for you and pour you out a blessing, that there shall not be room enough to receive it (*AMP*).

The Lord promises that as we give to Him, He will bless us. Even as He gives to us out of a Father's heart of unbounding love, He desires that we give to Him in the same manner, out of a cheerful willing spirit (see 2 Corinthians 9:7). As we will see in this chapter, there is more to stewardship than simply the management of finances.

A Closer Look at the Problem

A steward may be defined as "one who manages another's property or financial affairs; one who administers as the agent of another." We, as daughters of God our Father, are His agents. Part of our calling lies in the management of His property. But what *is* the Father's property as far as our lives are concerned? This chapter will help us learn how we can be good stewards of the things entrusted to our care.

Read 1 Corinthians 6:19-20. What areas in your life are mentioned here that should be regarded as God's property, but are not always acknowledged as such?

_____

_____

_____

_____

What other things in your life ought to be the Lord's, but are not?

_____

_____

_____

_____

A Closer Look at God's Truth

There are several areas of stewardship: time, talents, abilities and children.

STEWARDS OF OUR TIME

Read Colossians 4:5-6. How can we make the most of every opportunity?

_____

_____

_____

_____

_____

Write these verses in your own words, as they could be applied to your life right now.

_____

_____

_____

_____

Each day of our lives is precious for we live each day only once. Each hour— or moment—we choose whether we live in obedience to our Lord or squander that time by using it to please ourselves. Paul wrote, "So whether you eat or drink or whatever you do, do it all for the glory of God" (1 Corinthians 10:31). And David said, "My times are in your hands" (Psalm 31:15).

Read Ephesians 5:15-21. What are some things that we know are the will of God concerning the use of our time?

_____

_____

_____

_____

_____

Read Proverbs 31:10-31. Make a list of at least eight ways in which the godly woman depicted in these verses redeems her time.

_____

_____

_____

_____

_____

STEWARDS OF OUR TALENTS AND ABILITIES

Each of us has talents or gifts. Right now we are not considering the gifts of the Spirit but the natural abilities and talents each of us possess in some measure.

After God instructed Moses to build Him a tabernacle, according to Exodus 35:4-20, Moses asked the people to bring the materials needed to construct the tent. Not only did the people give so much that they had to be restrained from giving, they also gave of themselves.

As you read Exodus 35:4–36:2, answer the following questions:

What types of abilities did God give these women (see verses 25-26)?

_____

_____

_____

What types of skills and abilities did He give to Bezalel and Oholiab (see verses 30-35)?

_____

_____

_____

What else besides skill and ability was necessary to enable each person to do his or her job (see Exodus 36:1)?

_____

_____

_____

_____

_____

Who enabled these men and women to do the work God had called them to do (see Exodus 35:30-31,34-35)?

_____

_____

_____

_____

_____

How would you describe their attitude toward their tasks?

_____

_____

_____

_____

_____

What about you? You may be one who enjoys one or more of the following:

- creating lovely flower arrangements
- cooking a better-than-average meal
- designing a building
- organizing
- accounting
- counseling
- writing cheery or humorous notes
- raising vegetables
- teaching

The list is endless—almost everyone has a hobby or something she enjoys doing and does it well.

List two or three of your talents and abilities. They may be like those we have already considered, or they may be decidedly different.

_____

_____

_____

_____

Because you belong to your Father, your gifts and abilities belong to Him, too. However, you are a caretaker of these gifts. Is there some way in which your special ability could, when yielded to the Holy Spirit, meet a need in another's life? Simply doing something extra when we see a need that we are able to supply through our giftedness brings joy to our hearts. It also brings joy to the heart of God.

STEWARDS OF OUR CHILDREN'S LIVES
Read Psalms 127:3 and 128:3. What does the psalmist say about children?

_____

_____

_____

_____

Since all that we are and have is given to us out of the abundance of God's grace, we are also stewards of that most precious possession, our children. When you became a parent, God entrusted a life to you. You now have the privilege and responsibility of nurturing, educating and guiding this new life into spiritual truths, and the greatest privilege of all: leading your child to the saving knowledge of the Lord Jesus Christ.

Read Deuteronomy 6:6-9; Psalm 78:1-8 and 2 Timothy 1:5. Describe the responsibilities parents have in teaching their children the truths of God's Word.

_____

_____

_____

_____

Time, patience and faith are required to raise a child to the glory of God. Your children, under your prayers and guidance, need to grow and mature spiritually until they are able to take hold of the things of God for them-selves. Their mother's faith becomes their faith; her God, their God. Your children will leave home equipped with a foundation on which to build their lives as one yielded to the will of God.

As your children pass from your authority, discipline and guidance to that of their heavenly Father, you will keep the right of counsel and the privilege of praying. However, you are raising sons and daughters for the family of the King of kings. They have an eternal destiny with God in His kingdom that has been ordained before the foundation of the world.

Share examples of practical ways in which you can help make God real in a child's life.

_____

_____

_____

_____

As children grow older, their needs change. As a result, our ministry to them adjusts to meet their needs. Think of some ways in which your role and ministry to your child will change as he or she enters the young adult years. For example, how would you deal with a situation in which your child was experimenting with drugs or dating a non-Christian?

_____

_____

_____

_____

OTHER CHILDREN

Even if you do not have children of your own (or your children are grown), you can still have an impact on the lives of the children around you. You can build relationships with the children of other family members, friends or neighbors. You could be a Sunday School helper, be a listening ear for a lonely teenager, or become a Big Sister. There are opportunities all around you.

You might instead be blessed with spiritual children—new believers whom God has sent into your life. You could guide someone along the path toward spiritual maturity much like Paul nurtured Timothy (see 1 Timothy 1:2) and many others.

Consider your own childhood. Who had a life-changing impact on your life? What did he or she do to affect you?

_____

_____

_____

_____

In what ways could you have an eternal impact on the lives of children around you?

_____

_____

_____

_____

A WOMAN'S INFLUENCE
Twenty-five kings of Israel and Judah are listed in 1 and 2 Kings and 2 Chronicles. The Bible records the length of each reign, whether that particular king did good or evil in the sight of the Lord, and in the same verse, the name of each king's mother. Of such importance was the mother's influence on her son that Scripture has preserved each name. What a sacred trust God gives each of us in the management of His property and affairs!

A Closer Look at My Own Heart

What has God impressed upon your heart concerning your stewardship of your time, talents and resources?

_____

_____

_____

_____

Perhaps no area of stewardship weighs heavier on our hearts than that of our responsibility for the children in our lives. But children can also be the source of our greatest joy. They add a special relationship to our lives that no other relationship can equal. If you have no children of your own, you can "adopt" a niece or nephew or the child next door by becoming someone special in that child's life.

What ministry opportunities with children are there in your church or community? List them, and then prayerfully consider whether one of these is something you can do.

_____

_____

_____

_____

Action Steps I Can Take Today

On a separate piece of paper, write your thoughts and answers as you consider the following questions:

- *How can I redeem the time God gives to me each day? How can I cut down on wasted moments? What spiritual disciplines can I practice that will help me be more productive?* A brainstorming session with a friend might give you some additional ideas that you can implement.

- *How can I minister to others in my home and/or church through the stewardship of my special talent?* Spend time in prayer over each thought the Holy Spirit brings into your mind. Ask your prayer partner to pray with you. Also ask her for her ideas.

- *How can I begin now to help develop a strong, personal and enduring relationship between a child and the heavenly Father?* Jot down any ideas that come into your mind. Take time to pray about it this week. Expect God to direct your thoughts.

Read 2 Timothy 3:12-16. On a separate piece of paper, rewrite this passage as though you were writing to your son, your daughter or a young friend. Emphasize the same points that Paul does. Prayerfully consider giving your son, daughter or young friend the words you have written. If they are too young to understand now, save it and give it to them when they are older.

SIX

INISTERING IN CONVERSATION AND IN PEACE

PART ONE: MINISTERING IN CONVERSATION

A blow with a word strikes deeper than a blow with a sword.
ROBERT BURTON

As a child, did you ever chant, "Sticks and stones may break my bones, but words will never hurt me"? Although you may have chanted these words to ward off the hurtful words of a classmate or friend, from personal experience we know it is not true—unkind words can inflict wounds that cause pain long after the scars of physical wounds have healed.

Our words have the power to build up or tear down others. The quality of our conversation reflects the quality of our relationship with the Lord. This chapter will teach us how we can glorify our Father through our spoken words.

A Closer Look at the Problem

The book of James makes some penetrating statements on the subject of the tongue. One of them is that if anyone thinks herself to be religious—carefully observant of the external duties of her faith—and does not control her tongue, but deludes her own heart, this person's religious service is worthless (see James 1:26).

Do you agree or disagree with this statement: "It has been said that words once spoken can never be forgotten"? Explain your answer.

_____

_____

_____

_____

Read James 3:1-16. These verses present a graphic picture of the power of
the tongue and its potential for evil. But all is not lost. As we yield ourselves to the Holy Spirit, we begin to hear our own words. Although we
want to please the Father in our conversation, we know we do not always
do so. Rewrite verse 8 in your own words.

_____

_____

_____

What is the remedy to the dilemma of an uncontrolled tongue?

_____

_____

_____

_____

Even though James tells us we can't tame the tongue, we can yield it to the
control of the Holy Spirit. The goal of this chapter is to not only identify
the problem, but also to act on the truth we receive from God's Word.

A Closer Look at God's Truth

WISDOM FROM ABOVE

Proverbs 31:26 tells us that the godly woman opens her mouth with wisdom and gives faithful instruction. But what does wisdom look like? Read
the following references and answer the questions to discover the nature
of wisdom:

James 3:17-18. What do you discover about the fruit of wisdom?

_____

_____

_____

_____

Proverbs 3:13-15. How do we profit from gaining wisdom?

_____

_____

_____

_____

Proverbs 8:12-20. What are the attributes of wisdom?

_____

_____

_____

_____

Proverbs 8:22-36 and 1 Corinthians 1:23-24. Who is wisdom?

_____

_____

_____

_____

Colossians 2:2-3. What else do we possess when we gain wisdom?

_____

_____

_____

_____

Reread the references above, and then write your own description of wisdom.

_____

_____

_____

_____

_____

INSTRUCTIONS CONCERNING CONVERSATION

Psalms and Proverbs are rich in instruction on the subject of conversation. "The heart of the wise teaches [her] mouth, and adds learning to [her] lips" (Proverbs 16:23, *NKJV*). Under the guidance of the Holy Spirit within our hearts, we should be constantly instructing our mouths to speak only that which glorifies the Father, just as Jesus did (see John 12:50).

Read Proverbs 10:19 in several translations (*The Living Bible* is especially picturesque). What does this verse say about the person who talks too much?

_____

_____

_____

_____

Give an example from your own personal experience that proves this to be true.

_____

_____

_____

_____

_____

In Proverbs 31:26 (*NKJV*), describing the godly woman, what is your understanding of the phrase "law of kindness" (the *NIV* says "faithful instruction")?

_____

_____

_____

_____

_____

Can you identify with the godly woman in this verse? Why or why not?

_____

_____

_____

_____

_____

It has been said that we possess what we confess. "For it is with your heart that you believe and are justified, and it is with your mouth that you confess and are saved" (Romans 10:10). If we constantly talk about sickness, depression and negative things, then we either possess these things or they possess us. Scripture tells us, "For as [she] thinks in [her] heart, so is [she]" (Proverbs 23:7, *NKJV*).

WARNINGS ABOUT WORDS

Proverbs 18:20-21 warns us about the consequences of our words: "A *woman's* [moral] self shall be filled with the fruit of *her* mouth; and with the consequence of *her* words she must be satisfied [whether good or evil]. Death and life are in the power of the tongue, and they who indulge in it shall eat the fruit of it [for death or life]" (*AMP*, italics indicate author's substitution of feminine words for masculine).

Meditate on this passage, and then write it in your own words.

_____

_____

_____

_____

According to what you have written, in what way is the tongue responsible for life and death?

_____

_____

_____

_____

Scripture teaches us that our words carry everlasting consequences. If we yield to the Holy Spirit within, love becomes the source of the words that flow from our lips into the ears of our families, fellow Christians, neighbors and the world. Jesus said, "For out of the fullness (the overflow, the superabundance) of the heart the mouth speaks" (Matthew 12:34, _AMP_).

WARNINGS ABOUT JUDGING
According to James 4:11-12, why should we be careful to not judge another person?

_____

_____

_____

_____

Read Matthew 12:35-37. What do you think Matthew means by "every careless word they have spoken" (verse 36)?

_____

_____

_____

_____

What kind of power does our speech have over us?

_____

_____

_____

Read Romans 14:10-13. Where will this accounting of our spoken words take place?

_____

_____

_____

_____

_____

Read John 5:30 and Acts 10:42. Who alone has the right to judge?

_____

_____

_____

_____

_____

According to Romans 2:1-3, what are we doing to ourselves when we judge another (verse 1)?

_____

_____

_____

_____

What will be the results of our judgment of others (verse 3)?

Christians can easily fall into a habit of criticizing and judging others, thereby actually setting themselves in the place of God. According to Exodus 20:3, why is such an attitude considered so serious a sin in God's eyes?

_____

_____

_____

_____

Which commandment is being broken when we criticize or judge another person (see Exodus 20:2-17)?

_____

_____

_____

_____

Another area we need to be careful in is that of sharing prayer burdens concerning others' needs. It is easy to fall into gossip; therefore spiritual discernment must be exercised. "A talebearer reveals secrets, but he who is of a faithful spirit conceals a matter" (Proverbs 11:13, *NKJV*).

Read Proverbs 15:1 and Colossians 4:6. Give an example of what it means to season our speech with salt.

_____

_____

_____

_____

A Closer Look at My Own Heart

If you know of incidents when you have made critical or judgmental statements about someone, there is something you can do. You can follow God's directions for a clean heart by following the instructions given in 1 John 1:9. When you do confess, what does God promise to do?

_____

_____

_____

_____

WORDS OF GRACE

Ephesians 4:22-23 admonishes us to strip off the former nature and be constantly renewed in the spirit of our minds. And verse 25 continues, "putting away lying, 'Let each one of you speak truth with [her] neighbor,' for we are members of one another" (*NKJV*).

Since we belong to one another in the Body of Christ, we need to minister to one another by loving, encouraging and praying. One day the Church is going to be presented to Christ as a bride, without spot or wrinkle (see Ephesians 5:27).

Do you see any spots or wrinkles in the Body of Christ? We can be those who smooth out the wrinkles and remove the spots wherever we can. Ephesians 4:29 gives instructions:

Let no foul or polluting language, nor evil word nor unwholesome or worthless talk [ever] come out of your mouth, but only such [speech] as is good and beneficial to the spiritual progress of others, as is fitting to the need and the occasion, that it may be a blessing and give grace (God's favor) to those who hear it (*AMP*).

Have you ever known a person whose words refreshed you? Whose gracious and positive attitude uplifted and encouraged your heart? This is the kind of daughter God wants you to be.

You can become this kind of woman by choosing to start right where you are, at home, in your office or on the telephone. First, ask the Holy Spirit to make your ears sensitive to your own words as they come from your lips. Second, determine whether or not your words bring blessing to others and glory to God. Allow a day or two to experience this discipline of "listening" before completing the following action steps.

Action Steps I Can Take Today

Write down an example of how you yielded to the Holy Spirit in a conversation during your listening day. What was the result?

Use the following questions to help you examine your heart before your heavenly Father:

- As you disciplined your ears, were you content with what you heard coming from your mouth?
- What part of your conversation most needs to be brought under the Holy Spirit's control?
- Where is there need for further yieldedness within your spirit?

Are you willing to pray Psalm 141:3? If you are, then be encouraged. Your heavenly Father hears and answers prayers.

Write Psalm 141:3 on a 3x5-inch card. Read it each morning, and throughout the day as needed, as a prayer.

Part Two: Ministering in Peace

Our world cries out for peace. It is . . .

- Sought after by nations
- Talked about by the media
- Longed for by individuals

Is peace really possible? And if it is, how does it come about? When does it come? Can it be present in the midst of crisis, pain or sorrow?

One of the most beautiful pictures of peace known to mankind is the one painted by David in the Twenty-Third Psalm. Lush green grass, cool water, rest, oil for our wounds, a table spread with good things. But wait—enemies are present!

Peace in the presence of enemies? Yes, because God is there and He wants us to experience Jesus as our peace.

A Closer Look at the Problem

Our God is a God of peace. But because of Adam's sin passed on to the entire human race, our relationship with God was destroyed. The result was separation and death. Only God could restore us to the family relationship that He originally intended for us to enjoy.

This chapter will show us how to restore the fellowship and peace God has provided through Jesus Christ. Plunged into spiritual darkness as a result of sin, we need His light to show us His peace.

Because of and through the heart of tender mercy and loving-kindness of our God, a Light from on high will dawn upon us and visit [us] to shine upon and give light to those who sit in darkness and in the shadow of death, to direct and guide our feet in a straight line into the way of peace (Luke 1:78-79, *AMP*).

A Closer Look at God's Truth

Peace Through the Blood of the Lamb
According to John 1:4-9 and 9:5, who is the light that will guide our feet into the way of peace?

_____

_____

_____

Read Colossians 1:19-23. How does Jesus' death on the cross bring us into a relationship of peace with God?

_____

_____

_____

Read Leviticus 17:11 and Romans 3:23-26. Whose blood was put on the altar for the atonement of sin in the days of the Law? Whose blood did it represent?

_____

_____

_____

_____

Only the perfect sinless blood of the Son of God could meet God's holy standard. Jesus had to come and die in our place so that we would not all perish from "blood poisoning" (sin) but would have eternal life through faith in that once-for-all sacrifice.

Pretend that your name is Pauline and that you are writing a letter to a young Jewish Christian. Explain salvation to her in a simple way by rewriting Leviticus 17:11 and Romans 3:23-26 in your own words.

_____

_____

_____

_____

_____

THE PRINCE OF PEACE

Jesus is not *only* the Lamb of God who takes away the sin of the world, but He is also the Prince of Peace (see Isaiah 9:6). In Ephesians 2:13-14, Paul stated explicitly that there is no true peace outside of Jesus; we must have peace with God through salvation before we can experience the peace of God, that is, the outworking of His peace in our lives. As we yield to His Spirit, allowing His peace to manifest itself through us in the practical aspects of daily life, we begin to produce the fruit of the Spirit.

One aspect of the Spirit's work in us is to produce peace (see Galatians 5:22). Read Proverbs 12:20. What other fruit of the Spirit does the promoter of peace produce?

_____

_____

_____

_____

Read Romans 10:15. What does Paul say about those who proclaim the gospel of peace?

_____

_____

_____

_____

According to Matthew 5:9, what does Jesus call the peacemakers of our world?

_____

_____

_____

_____

CONSTANT PEACE

We live in times of anxiety and tension. The atmosphere is permeated with negative thoughts, coming from news broadcasts, the Internet, movies and general conversation. Although the Christian is not of the world (see John 17:15-16), she is in it and is constantly being bombarded by the fiery darts of Satan's realm.

However, Isaiah 26:3 promises, "You will guard him and keep him in perfect and constant peace whose mind [both its inclination and its character] is stayed on You, because he commits himself to You, leans on You, and hopes confidently in You" (*AMP*).

Do you think it is possible to have this kind of perfect and constant peace? Why, or why not?

_____

_____

_____

_____

Describe a situation in which you would like this passage to be real in your life.

_____

_____

_____

_____

PEACE IN CRISIS

Has something like the following ever happened to you? You are late getting home from work, the children have messed up the house, and you forgot to pick up margarine and milk. Dinner is thrown together and your husband is upset. What is your reaction? A headache? An anxiety attack? Or an underlying peace and calm because you know and confidently trust in Jesus, the Prince of Peace?

How does trusting God enable us to yield ourselves to Him?

_____

_____

_____

_____

Philippians 4:6-7 is a well-known Scripture passage about peace. Here is how the *Amplified Bible* states these verses: "Do not fret or have any anxiety about anything, but in every circumstance and in everything, by prayer and petition, (definite requests), with thanksgiving, continue to make your wants known to God. And God's peace [shall be yours, that tranquil state of a soul assured of its salvation through Christ, and so fearing nothing from God and being content with its earthly lot of whatever sort that is, that peace] which transcends all understanding shall garrison and mount guard over your hearts and minds in Christ Jesus."

Notice that this passage is in the form of a command. If the command is obeyed, a result is promised. Differentiating between your part and God's part will help you see what your responsibility is and what God's responsibility is in your pursuit of peace. Complete the following:

My Part	God's Part

The peace promised in this verse is not meant to be a once-in-a-lifetime experience, but an actual way of life. If we yield to Him and allow Him to live through us, then when crisis comes, we are already "fixed" in peace.

THE BLESSINGS OF PEACE

According to John 14:27, what do you think Jesus meant when He said, "I do not give to you as the world gives"?

_____

_____

_____

_____

_____

Read Psalm 4:8. When our spirits are peaceful, what is another blessing we will possess?

_____

_____

_____

_____

John 16:33 says, "I have told you these things, so that in Me you may have [perfect] peace and confidence. In the world you have tribulation and trials and distress and frustration; but be of good cheer [take courage; be confident, certain, undaunted]! For I have overcome the world. [I have deprived it of power to harm you and have conquered it for you]" (*AMP*). According to this verse, how do we know we can experience perfect peace in Jesus?

_____

_____

_____

_____

_____

MAINTAINING PEACE

A woman is often called to set a spiritual atmosphere in her home. This is true whether she is a fulltime homemaker or a career woman, married or single. Not only does it take wisdom to restore peace in the various relationships within the family, but also peace is in constant need of maintenance.

Give an example of something you can do today to maintain a peaceful climate in your home and at your job.

_____
_____
_____
_____

In what ways do Christians bring peace . . .

To the Church (see Ephesians 4:3)?

_____
_____
_____
_____

To the world (see Romans 10:15)?

_____
_____
_____
_____

Read James 3:17-18. When we pray for guidance and heavenly wisdom, how do we recognize it when it comes (verse 17)?

_____
_____
_____
_____

What kind of harvest do peacemakers reap (verse 18)?

_____
_____
_____
_____

God is not the author of confusion and disorder but of peace and order (see 1 Corinthians 14:33). This is true in the Church, in family and work relationships, and within our own hearts.

The woman "who wants to enjoy life and see good days" is advised to "keep *her* tongue free from evil and *her* lips from guile. . . . Let *her* turn away from wickedness and shun it, and let *her* do right. Let *her* search for peace (harmony; undisturbedness from fears, agitating passions, and moral conflicts) and seek it eagerly. [Do not merely desire peaceful relations with God, with your fellowmen, and with yourself, but pursue, go after them!]" (1 Peter 3:10-11, *AMP*, italics indicate author's substitution of feminine pronouns for masculine).

A Closer Look at My Own Heart

First Peter 3:4 gives further insight to women into the type of spirit we should possess if we want to please God: "But let it be the inward adorning and beauty of the hidden person of the heart, with the incorruptible and unfading charm of a gentle and peaceful spirit, which [is not anxious or wrought up, but] is very precious in the sight of God" (*AMP*).

Why do you think a gentle and peaceful spirit is so precious in God's sight?

_____

_____

_____

_____

What would you have to do in order to have a peaceful and gentle spirit?

_____

_____

_____

_____

Review the verses in this lesson, and meditate on the ones that are especially meaningful to you. Then make a list of qualities that should be evident in the life of a Christian woman who has made peace with God, her fellowmen and herself her goal.

_____

_____

_____

_____

Action Steps I Can Take Today

Prayerfully examine the list you made. Which quality do you sense that God wants you to develop?

What is one practical step you can take this week that will help you in your quest for peace?

Ask your prayer partner to pray for you and keep you accountable in what you have decided to do.

SEVEN

MINISTERING IN SUBMISSION AND HUMILITY

The emphasis of this study has been that of yieldedness: allowing Jesus to be Lord of our lives and giving Him the right to express Himself through us. We have been . . .

- Renewing our minds
- Unlearning old behavior patterns
- Tuning in to the Father's voice
- Studying what He desires
- Becoming sensitive to sin and to the joy of obedience

A Closer Look at the Problem

In this chapter we will look again at yieldedness, or submission, that quality of humility that is so important to the spiritual life. Keep in mind that submission is a proper attitude before God and others. Often misunderstood or questioned, it is the basis, or root, of all things spiritual.

Someone has said, either bend in submission or break in rebellion. Do you agree or disagree with this statement? Explain your position.

_____

_____

_____

_____

A Closer Look at God's Truth

WHAT DID JESUS SAY?

The New Testament is not only a narrative of Jesus' relationship with the Father, but also a pattern for us to follow in our personal relationships with God. Our study begins by looking at Jesus as our example of submission. Read the following verses and write what Jesus says about Himself:

John 5:19

_____

_____

_____

_____

John 5:30

_____

_____

_____

_____

John 5:41

_____

_____

_____

_____

John 6:38

_____

_____

_____

_____

John 7:16

_____

_____

_____

_____

John 8:50

_____

_____

_____

_____

John 14:10

_____

_____

_____

_____

These statements are only examples of the many times Jesus spoke of His total submission to the Father. In His perfect humanity, Jesus set the pattern as He consistently chose to submit and depend on His heavenly Father.

WHAT DID JESUS DO?
Read Philippians 2:1-8. Rewrite verses 6-8 in your own words.

_____

_____

_____

_____

What one word describes Jesus' attitude?

_____

_____

_____

_____

What does the Father expect from us (verse 5)?

_____

_____

_____

What do we learn in these verses about who Christ is?

_____

_____

_____

_____

The one true God has always existed as God the Father, Jesus Christ the Son, and the Holy Spirit. This is a side-by-side relationship, no one being greater or lesser than the other; all flow together in union, yet each one has distinctive qualities and functions.

How Does the Father Glorify the Son?
Read Philippians 2:9-11. What did the Father do for Christ as a result of His humbling of Himself even to death on the cross?

Philippians 2:9

_____
_____
_____
_____

Philippians 2:10

_____
_____
_____
_____

What is the end result of His sacrifice and the exaltation that follows (see verse 11)?

_____
_____
_____
_____

How Does Jesus Glorify the Father?
Everything Jesus thought, did, spoke and taught was focused toward one all-encompassing goal: to glorify God, His Father. What is the purpose, the motivation of your life at this time?

_____
_____
_____
_____

How does it compare with Christ's goal of glorifying the Father?

_____
_____
_____
_____

Jesus always obeyed the Father, even to the shameful, agonizing death at Calvary. Now we belong twice to Him: first, by creation, and second, bought back from Satan by Jesus' shed blood.

How Do We Glorify the Son?

Read Romans 12:1-2 and 1 Corinthians 6:20. As a result of the great price Jesus paid for us, what should we choose to do (verse 20)?

_____

_____

_____

_____

Read these verses in several translations if possible, and then write down how you can glorify God in your body.

_____

_____

_____

_____

Isaiah 66:2 is a description of the type of person God esteems. Do you know someone who has these qualities? How do his or her words and actions reveal humility?

_____

_____

_____

_____

How can you develop the heart qualities described in this verse?

_____

_____

_____

_____

According to 1 Peter 5:5-6, who is to submit to whom?

_____

_____

_____

_____

What do you think is meant by the phrase "clothe yourselves with humility"?

_____

_____

_____

_____

_____

How does God feel about the sin of pride?

_____

_____

_____

_____

_____

From your knowledge of God, why do you think He hates pride so much?

_____

_____

_____

_____

_____

What does He give the humble?

_____

_____

_____

_____

_____

Review John 13:1-17; 14:2 and Ephesians 13:3-5,18-19. What did Jesus know about Himself, and what do we know about ourselves in our relationship to God that makes us so secure that it is possible to deliberately and joyfully choose the way of humility and graciousness?

_____

_____

_____

_____

_____

SUBMISSION AND OBEDIENCE

According to Ephesians 1:22-23, who is the spiritual head and authority over the Church?

_____

_____

_____

_____

As a result of the Church's submission to Christ, what will be its final state (see Ephesians 5:27)?

_____

_____

_____

_____

_____

Through these lessons we have seen again and again how much our Lord desires our obedience. He desires to reward and exalt us even as He has rewarded and exalted His Son.

A PATTERN TO FOLLOW

Read Ephesians 5:22-29. What is the pattern of submission in verses 22 and 24?

_____

_____

_____

_____

Why is submission such a difficult concept for many women to accept today?

_____

_____

_____

_____

Even though our culture has caused many women to view submission as a red flag, this is not God's intention. He desires that the relationship of the submissive wife to her husband be a picture or symbol to the non-Christian of the Church's relationship, as the Bride, to Jesus Christ, her Bridegroom.

What balance is given in the following verses from Ephesians 5?

Ephesians 5:25

_____

_____

_____

_____

_____

Ephesians 5:28

_____

_____

_____

_____

Ephesians 5:31

_____

_____

_____

_____

Ephesians 5:33

_____

_____

_____

_____

As a parallel to the wife's submission, the husband is to be a picture of Christ, the Bridegroom, who loves His beloved, the Church, so much that He died for her.

Our submission to our husbands does not make us second-class citizens. As viewed by God, we have a side-by-side relationship with our spouses. He views us as equally important, but each of us is designed to function for His glory, in his or her own role. We saw this earlier exemplified in the Trinity—Father, Son, Spirit: equal, united, flowing together, completing one another even as we are meant to do in the role of marriage.

Read 1 Peter 3:1-6. What other reason does the Lord have for married women to be submissive to their husbands?

_____

_____

_____

_____

How did Sarah and other women make themselves beautiful (verse 4)?

_____

_____

_____

_____

Sarah knew nothing of Christ dying for His Bride, the Church, yet she willingly placed herself in submission to Abraham even to the point of calling him her master.

_____

_____

_____

_____

What do we have in common with the women of old that will help us make the right decisions (verse 5)?

_____

_____

_____

_____

According to Ephesians 5:21, to whom, whether we are single or married, are we to have a submissive attitude?

_____

_____

_____

_____

God does not desire to humble us, although at times chastisement for disobedience is necessary. He desires that each of us make the choice even as Jesus Himself did.

We read in Philippians 2:8 that Jesus deliberately chose to humble Himself. In Luke 14:7-11 we learn that Jesus desires that we, too, humble ourselves. As you meditate on these verses, ask yourself, *What will be the result in my lifestyle if I choose to humble myself?*

A Closer Look at My Own Heart

Shortly before He went to the cross, Jesus told His disciples that the hour had come for Him to be glorified (see John 12:23-26). In these verses Jesus likened a seed falling to the ground and dying to that of His death and burial. The seed springing forth and living again to produce many seeds illustrates His resurrection.

This dying seed is a beautiful symbol of Christ's submission and exaltation. It also symbolizes our death to self and our coming alive in the power of the Holy Spirit.

The entire Christian life is to be a submitted life. Over and over, the Scriptures teach us to:

- Honor one another above ourselves (see Romans 12:10)
- Consider others better than ourselves (see Philippians 2:3)
- Build up one another (see Ephesians 4:29; 1 Thessalonians 5:11)
- Love and esteem our Christian brothers and sisters (see Romans 12:10; Ephesians 4:32; Hebrews 13:1; 1 Peter 3:8)

Action Steps I Can Take Today

What is one area in your life in which you need to submit to God?

How then will you choose to live? Complete the following prayer:

Lord Jesus, in the best way I know how, I submit to You . . .

Consider how you could help another believer. Prayerfully ask God to reveal a situation or relationship in which you can serve, honor or encourage another believer.

EIGHT

MINISTERING LOVE

"Love" is one of the most overused words in the English language. In a single conversation the word might be used for anything ranging from a love for nuts or a current movie to the love for a pet, a child or God.

The Greeks, however, had four words denoting love: *storgos*, a natural affection, as in a parent for a child, or an animal for its offspring; *eros*, a passion seeking satisfaction (not found in the New Testament); *philia*, a friendly or brotherly love based on mutual attraction; *agape*, an awakened sense of value and preciousness in an object causing one to prize and highly esteem it. This latter word occurs more than 300 times in the New Testament.

A Closer Look at the Problem

We have learned in this study that the daughter of God can grow into spiritual maturity only as she yields to the indwelling Holy Spirit. It is the same with love.

The *agape* love of the Christian discussed in this chapter can no more be achieved as a result of self-discipline or resolution than can spiritual maturity. This, our final lesson in this series, expresses the heart of God: "For God so loved the world that he gave his one and only Son" (John 3:16).

Paul stated in Romans 5:5, "God has poured out his love into our hearts by the Holy Spirit, whom he has given us." God's love works in and through the Christian. We cannot *produce* divine love; we *experience* it as an indwelling Person. Only as His love flows unobstructed through our hearts can we express His glory.

A Closer Look at God's Truth

"CHRIST IN ME"
Read 1 Corinthians 13. Everywhere the English word "love" is found in this chapter, the Greek word *agape* is used. As you read, substitute "Christ

in me" for the word "love." Only as we submit to the indwelling Spirit of Jesus can we experience His love.

Reread verse 13. Why do you think the greatest of these is love?

_____

_____

_____

_____

_____

Read 1 Peter 1:22. The first time the word "love" is used, the Greek word is *philadelphia*, which means brotherly love (combining *philia* and *adelphos*, meaning "brother"); the second time, the verb form of *agape* is used. Rephrase this verse by differentiating between the two kinds of love.

_____

_____

_____

_____

_____

LOVING OTHERS

Read Luke 10:25-37 and 1 Thessalonians 3:12. When the young lawyer asked Jesus, "Who is my neighbor?" Jesus answered with the story of the Good Samaritan. Based on the teaching in these verses, who is your neighbor?

_____

_____

_____

_____

Another time, Jesus said to His disciples, "And so I am giving a new commandment to you now—love each other just as much as I love you. Your strong love [*agape*] for each other will prove to the world that you are my disciples" (John 13:34-35, *TLB*).

Jesus gave the world the right to judge Christians on the basis of their observable love for one another. In other words, the world can judge whether or not we are true believers by the love they see us manifest for other Christians. Our love expressed toward other Christians is a testimony to the world.

Read Galatians 6:2 and Ephesians 4:32. These verses reveal some qualities about love that are not listed in 1 Corinthians 13. What are they?

_____

_____

_____

_____

Is there a particular situation in your family (or other relationship) where a work of love needs to be accomplished in and through you? Describe what needs to be done.

_____

_____

_____

_____

According to Matthew 5:43-48, who else are we to love?

_____

_____

_____

_____

Perhaps you don't think you have any enemies, but who are the people in your life that rub you the wrong way?

_____

_____

_____

_____

How do you react to those who have different social, moral and political views from yours?

_____

_____

_____

_____

Every morning our prayer needs to be, "Jesus, let me be such a channel of blessing that today, through me, You will love each person with whom I come into contact."

How Will You Love?
Read John 21:15-19. These somewhat baffling verses become clear when
we understand the Greek verbs used here for "love." When Jesus asks Peter if he loves Him, He uses the verb form of the highest form of love:
agape.

In essence Jesus asked, "Peter, do you have love (*agape*) for Me completely? Do you esteem Me highly enough to surrender yourself to Me?"

Twice He asked this and twice Peter replied, "Yes, Lord. You know I
have brotherly fondness (*philos*) for You."

The third time Jesus used Peter's word for love. "Peter, do you have
love (*philos*) for Me at all?" And Peter, grieved, can only answer, "Yes, Lord,
I have affection for You."

Right now, how would you answer the Lord if He asked the same question
of you?

_____

_____

_____

_____

_____

Who Will You Love?
The world is judging us on the basis of our observable love, not only indi-
vidually one to another, but also in our groups and denominations.

Read 1 Peter 3:8a. From this first portion of the verse, what manifestation
of love should be evident in every person, group or denomination?

_____

_____

_____

_____

_____

The love of Jesus flowing through us is a unifying factor, healing, bind-
ing and building up the Body of Christ. "Fill up and complete my joy by
living in harmony and being of the same mind and one in purpose, having
the same love, being in full accord and of one harmonious mind and intention" (Philippians 2:2, *AMP*).

Read Philippians 2:11. What is it that unifies us as we worship with believers of other denominations or doctrinal beliefs?

_____

_____

_____

_____

_____

Read John 17:21. If the world can observe love within the Church—whose strength springs from its unity in Christ Jesus—what will be the world's ultimate realization?

_____

_____

_____

_____

_____

Jesus desires that not only will the world know we are Christians by our love, but also that the Father did indeed send the Son.

A Closer Look at My Own Heart

CHOOSING TO LOVE

If you do not apply the spiritual truths presented in this study with *agape* love as the motivating factor, you are studying and ministering in vain. Service to God or hospitality from a heart attitude of duty rather than love is without eternal value. You may even manifest the gifts of the Spirit, but if love is absent, they are meaningless (see 1 Corinthians 13:1-2).

When you sense a lack of love in your heart, remember the two aspects of love: There is a love that springs from the emotions and fluctuates with changing moods and the volition (will), and there is a love that comes from a moral commitment to express unconditional love. A definition of *agape* love is "choosing its object with decision and self-denying compassion." This love has its source in God. The verb form has reference to the "tendency of the will." If you are to love the Father and others with all your heart, it is because you choose to allow His love to flow through you.

Give an example in your life in which, with God's grace, you must willfully choose to allow God's love to be expressed through you toward another person.

_____

_____

_____

_____

A PRAYER FOR YOU TO PRAY

Heavenly Father, lover of my soul, more than anything I long for Your love to flow through me, but I'm weak. And sometimes I don't even want to love, at least not in the way You said You want me to.

Change me, Father. Cleanse me. Make me into a clean vessel so that I can overflow to the world.

Help me to know that when I'm overflowing, I'm growing in love, even if it is just a little at a time. I'm maturing, developing in my Christian walk. I'm pressing forward to the goal of being like Christ by yielding to the Holy Spirit.

I love You, Father. You are my life, my love, the One I trust. Thank You for choosing me to be Your daughter.

In Jesus' name, amen.

Action Steps I Can Take Today

As you complete this study, remember this: You are created to be the daughter of the Most High God, created as a vessel through whom the Spirit of Jesus flows. This is our prayer for you:

May the Lord make you to increase and excel and overflow in love for one another and for all people, just as we also do for you. So that He may strengthen and confirm and establish your hearts faultlessly pure and unblamable in holiness in the sight of our God and Father, at the coming of our Lord Jesus Christ, (the Messiah) with all His saints (the holy and glorified people of God)! Amen (so be it)! (1 Thessalonians 3:12-13, AMP).

A WOMAN
AFTER GOD'S HEART
LEADER'S GUIDE

The purpose of this leader's guide is to provide those willing to lead a group Bible study with additional material to make the study more effective. Each lesson has one or two exercises designed to increase participation and lead the group members into closer relationship with their heavenly Father.

Each of the exercises are designed to introduce the study and emphasize the theme of the chapter. When two exercises are suggested, it is up to your discretion whether to use them both. Time will probably be the deciding factor.

If the group is larger than six members, you may want to break into smaller groups for the discussion time so that all will have an adequate opportunity to share. As the lessons proceed, the exercises will invite more personal sharing. Keep these two important points in mind:

1. Involve each member of the group in the discussion when at all possible. Some may be too shy or new to the Bible study experience. Be sensitive to their needs and encourage them to answer simple questions that do not require personal information or biblical knowledge. As they get more comfortable in the group, they will probably share more often.

2. Make a commitment with the group members that what is shared in the discussion times and prayer requests must be kept in strictest confidence.

After each lesson, be prepared to pray with those who have special needs or concerns. Emphasize the truth of God's Word as you minister to the group members, which will lead them to a closer relationship with their Lord and Savior.

ONE

S A FIT VESSEL

Objective

To help group members understand the need to be yielded to the Father, Son and Holy Spirit.

Preparation

EXERCISE

Obtain or make a yield traffic sign. (One possible source is from a primary school teacher or a teacher supply store, or you could take a photo of one and enlarge it.)

DISCUSSION

Familiarize yourself with the discussion questions included in the following "Group Participation" section, or choose which questions in this week's study you want to discuss with the group. Note that there might not be time to discuss every question, so modify or adapt this discussion guide as it fits the needs of your group. Additional discussion/action steps are also provided to help stimulate further discussion if you have the time.

Group Participation

EXERCISE

Display the Yield traffic sign and discuss the following questions:

1. What is this sign? (*A traffic sign.*)

2. When you see it along the street, what does it mean? (*It means watch out for oncoming traffic and let them go first.*)

3. What might happen if you don't obey this sign? (*An accident, injury, ticket, and so forth.*)

4. What would happen if you couldn't read English know what this sign said or what it meant? (*You would disobey it and cause an accident.*)

5. How does that relate to yielding to God?

Lead the discussion to yielding to God and the cost of disobeying His directions. Make the point that the only way we can know what God wants us to do is to be in communication with Him through prayer and reading His Word. Invite group members to share their definitions of yielding from this week's lesson.

DISCUSSION

1. Discuss the following questions (or the ones you chose) from the "A Closer Look at God's Truth" section:

   - Read Jesus' prayer for His followers in John 17:20-23. What kind of relationship does Jesus want us to have with Himself and the Father?

   - As we yield or flow with Him, what divine purpose is accomplished for the world to see?

   - What will be evident in our lives that will cause the world to know that the Father has indeed sent the Son?

   - This re-educating process takes place as one enters the school of the Spirit. Why, according to Isaiah 55:8, do we have difficulty in transforming our mindsets to God's mindset?

   - Give some examples of other scriptural principles that are opposed to our human reasoning (see Matthew 16:25; 20:26-27 to begin with).

ADDITIONAL DISCUSSION /ACTION STEPS

1. Read the warning at the end of the "A Closer Look at My Own Heart" section. Discuss what changes of attitude, conversation and/or activity might result from being yielded to the Holy Spirit. Invite group members to share their own experiences of how they have changed when yielding to the Father, Son and Holy Spirit.

...if any of the members has ever had an experience with a clogged sewer or septic system. What happened in his or her house because of the clog? How does that relate to when we allow sin to clog up our lives?

3. Ask members to comment on what is the ultimate purpose of being yielded to the Father, Son and Holy Spirit. Lead members to discover that our purpose is to carry on the work of Jesus here on earth and to bring God glory (see Matthew 5:14-16).

4. Discuss in what ways our yielding to the Lord can be a light to others.

5. Encourage group members to do the activities in the Action Steps section. If they have not already done so, have them pair up with another group member as a prayer partner to keep them accountable.

IN THE SPIRIT AND IN THE WORD

Objective

To help group members understand the functions of the Holy Spirit and God's Word in helping believers grow in spiritual maturity.

Preparation

EXERCISE 1

Prepare seven sheets of poster board by writing the fruit of the Spirit of Galatians 5:22-23 in acrostic form down the sides of each sheet of poster board (*Note*: "love," "joy" and "peace" could be written on one sheet). Obtain pens or pencils. (As an alternate exercise, obtain sheets of unlined paper and pens or pencils.)

EXERCISE 2

Gather several different kinds of instruction manuals. Try to find a variety, such as a car manual, a home appliance manual, an installation manual for something like a ceiling fan or light or a computer, a manual for a cell phone, and the like. If at all possible, find a few manuals that go with something that is obsolete, such as an old-style cell phone, TV or VHS recorder. If possible, find one sample manual for each group member (although this is not absolutely necessary as members could share manuals). An alternative way to obtain manuals is to call group members during the week and ask if they could bring a manual or two for this session.

DISCUSSION

Familiarize yourself with the discussion questions included in the following "Group Participation" section, or choose which questions in this week's study you want to discuss with the group.

Group Participation

EXERCISE 1

Form smaller groups of two to four members, depending on the size of your group. Give each small group one of the prepared poster boards. Tell the groups that they will be given about 10 minutes to write an acrostic that describes their assigned word. When the 10 minutes are up, instruct them to stop even if they are not done. Invite the small groups to read their acrostics aloud to the whole group.

ALTERNATE EXERCISE

Distribute one sheet of paper to each group member. Instruct them to write out the acrostic that they did at the end of Part One of this week's lesson. Tell them not to put their names on the papers. Give them a couple of minutes to do this, and then have them hand the papers to you. Mix the papers up and read a few as time allows. Discuss the following:

1. Why do you suppose this list of qualities is called the "fruit" (singular form) of the Spirit and not the "fruits" (plural form) of the Spirit? (*Believers are supposed to exhibit all of these qualities, not just some of them.*)

2. What is our responsibility in developing the fruit of the Spirit? (*Obedience, knowing God's Word, and so forth.*)

3. What is the Holy Spirit's role in developing the fruit of the Spirit in believers? (*Providing the strength and the ability to do what is needed, teaching us, and so forth.*)

EXERCISE 2

Give an instruction manual to each group member. If the group is large, give one to every two to three people and ask them to share the manual. Ask the following questions:

1. What have I just given you?

2. How many of you faithfully read the instruction manuals to everything you buy?

3. How many of you usually ignore the instruction manuals—at least until you run into a problem?

4. What is the purpose of these instruction manuals? (*To help us learn how to operate and maintain the item, for safety and repair information, and so forth.*)

5. How do manuals outlive their usefulness? Do any of you have a manual that you think is no longer useful? Why?

Conclude by comparing how the instruction manuals are similar to God's Word. Then ask how God's Word is different from these instruction manuals. Accept their answers and then, if no one else has mentioned it, point out that God's Word is never obsolete.

DISCUSSION

1. Discuss the following questions (or the ones you chose) from Part One of this week's study:

   - Explain how you have found this presence of God's power after a time of testing to be evident in your life or in the lives of others.

   - Read Romans 8:28-29. Why are testings and problems allowed in the lives of Christians?

   - According to 1 John 1:9, what does God promise us when we confess our sins to Him?

   - According to Isaiah 1:19 and Micah 6:8, what qualities does the Lord require of you, His daughter?

   - Evaluate your spiritual maturity while reading and meditating on Galatians 5:22-23 and 2 Peter 1:5-8. What character traits/qualities are produced by the Holy Spirit when we live a life of obedience?

2. Discuss the following questions (or the ones you chose) from Part Two of this week's study:

   - Read Exodus 16:4-36 and John 6:48-58. Explain in your own words how the life-giving manna was like Christ.

   - According to 2 Timothy 3:16-17, how does Scripture help us grow into spiritual maturity?

- Read 1 Corinthians 2:12 and 2 Timothy 3:17. For what purpose has Scripture and the Spirit been given?

- In Psalm 119:11, David states, "I have hidden your word in my heart that I might not sin against you." What do you think David meant by this statement?

- How could you apply these words to your own heart?

ADDITIONAL DISCUSSION/ACTION STEPS

1. In what ways do the Holy Spirit and the Word work together in a believer's life?

2. What does each produce in our lives?

3. What is one new thing you learned about the Holy Spirit in this week's lesson?

4. What is one new thing that you learned about the Word in this week's lesson?

5. What are some practical ways you can incorporate God's Word into your everyday life?

THREE

ℳINISTERING PRAISE

Objective

To help group members understand the what, where, when, how and why of praising the Lord and to give members an opportunity to express praises to the Lord.

Preparation

EXERCISE 1

Obtain five sheets of poster board. At the top of each sheet write one of the following phrases so that there is a different phrase on each poster board: "For What Reasons Do We Praise?" "Where We Praise," "When We Praise," "How We Praise" and "Why We Praise." Gather felt-tip pens and tape or tacks. Tape or tack the poster boards around the room. If that is not possible, the poster boards may be passed around the room or laid on tables.

EXERCISE 2

Invite someone—preferably one of the group members—who could lead the group in singing two or three praise and worship songs, or obtain a worship CD and player or an MP3 player. This will be used at the end of the session.

ALTERNATE WORSHIP IDEA

During the week, call each group member and encourage each person to create a unique way to worship the Lord, such as writing or reciting a poem or psalm of praise, creating a dance of praise, drawing a picture, taking a photo, presenting a brief slide show, playing or singing a worship song, or sharing some handiwork. Encourage the members to think of a way that uniquely expresses their praises to the Lord.

DISCUSSION

Familiarize yourself with the discussion questions included in the following "Group Participation" section, or choose which questions in this week's study you want to discuss with the group. Note that if you choose to do exercise 2 above, you will want to leave about 10 to 15 minutes at the end of the session for a time of praise and worship, so choose just the number of questions that you think your group will be able to discuss during the meeting time.

Group Participation

EXERCISE I

As group members enter the room, invite them to take a felt-tip pen and write one example for each phrase. Encourage them to be creative in their responses, but if the group is large, they can repeat some responses. When everyone is (or the majority are) done writing their responses, have five volunteers each take a poster board and share some of the responses on their board.

DISCUSSION

1. Discuss the following questions (or the ones you chose) from the "A Closer Look at God's Truth" section:

    · Read Deuteronomy 10:21; 1 Chronicles 16:34; 1 Peter 1:3; 2:9 and Revelation 5:12-14. What reasons are given for worshiping God?

    · Read Psalms 57:6-7; 108:1. Despite the distressing situation of his life, what was David's attitude?

    · According to 1 Peter 2:9, what are four reasons we should praise God?

    · Read Hebrews 13:15. Why do you think the word "sacrifice" is used in conjunction with praising?

    · Read Jonah 2:1-10. In Jonah's case, what was the result of his sacrifice of praise?

2. Read Ephesians 1:12. Ask the group what God' purpose is for each believer based on this verse.

EXERCISE 2
Close this session with a time of praise. Begin with a time of group prayer, inviting several members to call out brief praises to the Lord. Conclude by singing praise and worship songs.

ALTERNATE WORSHIP EXPERIENCE
Begin the worship time with prayer, and then invite volunteers to uniquely express their praises. Some may be shy or feel that the way they express praise is less acceptable than others, but encourage them that the Lord is the audience and that any praise is acceptable to Him.

$\mathcal{M}$INISTERING SERVICE AND HOSPITALITY

Objective

To help group members understand the importance of serving and showing hospitality to others.

Preparation

EXERCISE 1

Prepare to do a foot-washing service with group members. You will need one plastic dishpan for approximately every four to five group members, a towel for every member, plastic pitchers, a mild soap (such as Ivory), and large tubs or a nearby sink to provide water and a place to throw out used water. You could ask group members to supply some of these items. If you plan on doing this exercise, it is suggested that you contact group members beforehand so they can wear appropriate clothing. Some may want to opt out for various reasons. If they do, ask them to perform another job, such as emptying or filling wash basins, providing dry towels, and so forth. *Optional*: Obtain a worship CD and player or an MP3 player.

Set up the meeting room (or a separate room) with chairs arranged in a circle. If you have a large group, arrange several smaller circles. If you do not have easy access to a sink, you will need to have water provided in large tubs for dispensing water and then empty tubs to throw out the used water. Demonstrate how to do the foot washing by doing it for the first person in the circle. When you have washed that person's feet, hug him or her, and then that person will wash the next person's feet. Having someone else there to empty the dishpan and another to fill it with fresh water will help move this activity along.

EXERCISE 2

Obtain a whiteboard, chalkboard or flipchart.

DISCUSSION

Due to the length of this particular lesson, you will especially need to rely on the Lord's guidance in discerning what questions to emphasize during your discussion time. Familiarize yourself with the discussion questions included in the following "Group Participation" section, or choose which questions in this week's study you want to discuss with the group.

Group Participation

EXERCISE 1

Read John 13:1-15, and do the foot washing. You can play worship music while the foot washing is taking place or encourage the women to sing as the members wash each other's feet. When you are done, discuss the experience by asking the following questions:

1. What were your thoughts as you were having your feet washed?
2. What were your thoughts as you were washing another member's feet?
3. Why do you suppose Jesus washed His disciples' feet?
4. What are your thoughts on this action of Jesus?

EXERCISE 2

Invite group members to tell you those things, actions or elements that have helped them feel welcomed into someone else's home. List their comments on the board or flipchart. List what is most important in showing hospitality, such as a person's attitude, ability to make others feel comfortable, or choice to spend more time with his or her guests than in the kitchen. List those things that are not important in being hospitable, such as having a model perfect home, cooking gourmet meals, and so forth. Hopefully, you can point to the times in the first list to illustrate what it is that makes people feel welcomed.

DISCUSSION

1. As time allows, discuss the following questions (or the ones you chose) from Part One of the study:

   - Read John 13:1-17. This passage often describes the great servant-heart of our Lord. As you read it, pay special attention to verse 3. Write down three important facts that Jesus knew about Himself before He began to wash the disciples' feet.

- According to Ephesians 1:3-5,18-19 and John 14:2, what are we promised because of our relationship with Christ?

- What was Jesus trying to teach His disciples in John 12:23-26?

- Read John 12:26. As we flow together in Christ and He is in us ministering to others, what will the Father do?

- Read Revelation 22:3. What else besides praising and rejoicing will we be doing in heaven?

2. As time allows, discuss the following questions (or the ones you chose) from Part Two of the study:

- Read 1 Kings 17:7-24. What was the attitude of this widow toward Elijah and toward the Lord?

- Read 2 Kings 4:8-37. What are the differences in the circumstances surrounding the home of the widow of Zarephath and the Shunammite woman?

- Read Joshua 2:1-23. In what way was she rewarded for this ministry to them (see Joshua 6:20-25)?

- Why should we be diligent to practice hospitality toward the people who come to our homes?

- The dictionary defines "hospitality" as "the reception and entertainment of guests or strangers with generosity and kindness." On a scale of 1 to 10 (with 1 being poor and 10 being excellent), how would you rate your home in the ministry of hospitality?

ADDITIONAL DISCUSSION/ACTION STEPS

1. Ask the members in what ways others have served them.

2. Ask what it means to be a servant-leader. How was Jesus our example? (*For example, a servant-leader is more concerned with the needs of others and is kind and compassionate. Jesus served His disciples and the people in need all*

around them. He was more concerned for them than Himself. Ultimately He gave His life for us when we were yet sinners.)

3. Discuss in what ways hospitality serves others. (*Answers could include by making them feel welcome, by giving unbelievers an opportunity to enjoy Christian fellowship and a glimpse of Christ's love, by providing food and lodging to someone in need, and so forth.*)

4. Sometimes it is not possible to show hospitality to others in our own homes. Ask the members to suggest some creative ways that they can practice hospitality outside of their homes. (*For example, by greeting newcomers to their church and inviting them to join your group of friends, by inviting someone on a picnic or a hike, by inviting someone to lunch, by asking them to come to Bible study, or by taking a meal to someone in need.*)

FIVE

MANAGING THE FATHER'S AFFAIRS

Objective

To help group members become aware of the many ways they can be good stewards of the time, talents, bodies, materials, opportunities—everything—with which God has blessed them.

Preparation

EXERCISE 1

Obtain several 9 x 12-inch sheets of construction paper and felt-tip pens. You will also need a timer or watch with a second hand. *Optional*: Obtain a bag of candy or other treat for the winning team.

EXERCISE 2

Have a whiteboard, chalkboard or flipchart available. Beforehand, contact the church office and/or several ministries in your church or community and ask for specific ways that they need help. Write these ministry opportunities on the board or flipchart. Also prepare a list of these ministry needs on a handout.

DISCUSSION

Familiarize yourself with the discussion questions included in the following "Group Participation" section, or choose which questions in this week's study you want to discuss with the group. Again, if you choose to do exercise 2 above, you will want to leave about 10 to 15 minutes at the end of the session for a time of praise and worship, so choose just the number of questions that you think your group will be able to discuss during the meeting time.

Group Participation

EXERCISE 1

Divide the members into smaller groups of six to eight. Give each group a sheet of construction paper and a felt-tip pen. Tell them that they will have one minute to list the many things over which the Lord has given us stewardship. Instruct them to think creatively. Set the timer or consult your watch and tell them to begin. After one minute, call time and have them count their items. The group with the most items will read their list first. Other groups will then be given the opportunity to read items from their lists that the other groups did not mention. In case of a tie, the group with the most items unique to their list is declared the winner. Or you can give everyone a prize and declare them all winners!

EXERCISE 2

This exercise could be used as an alternate for the opening exercise or as a concluding exercise. Invite group members to share one ability or resource for which they discovered they need to be better stewards and then display the list of ministries that you have put together during the week. Challenge the group as a whole to take on a project, or challenge individuals to commit to fulfilling a role in one of these ministries. Give each member a copy of the list of ministries you have prepared. If they are not ready to commit at this point, instruct them to take the list home and prayerfully consider where they might serve. Challenge them to explore other possibilities if none of these opportunities fit their abilities. (Note: Some of your members may already be heavily involved in ministries. If so, challenge them to evaluate their various responsibilities to make sure they are making the best use of their time, talents and resources.)

DISCUSSION

Discuss the following questions (or the ones you chose) from this study:

- Read Colossians 4:5-6. How can we make the most of every opportunity?
- Read Ephesians 5:15-21. What are some things that we know are the will of God concerning the use of our time?
- Read Proverbs 31:10-31. Make a list of at least eight ways in which the godly woman depicted in these verses redeems her time.

- List two or three of your talents and abilities. They may be like those we have already considered, or they may be decidedly different.

- Read Psalms 127:3 and 128:3. What does the psalmist say about children?

- Share examples of practical ways in which you can help make God real in a child's life.

- Consider your own childhood. Who had a life-changing impact on your life? What did he or she do to affect you?

SIX

MINISTERING IN CONVERSATION AND IN PEACE

Objective

To help group members understand how our words can hurt or build up others and realize that true peace in difficult times comes only from reliance on God.

Preparation

EXERCISE 1

Contact group members during the week and ask them to think of some funny conversational missteps that are perhaps a part of their family lore. It could be something a child has said or a twisting of words that had hilarious results. If they cannot think of anything (or don't want to embarrass family members), ask them to think of something a celebrity might have said—something for which everyone remembers that person. Ask them to write out the incident and prepare to share it during the session. Collect some of your own stories as well.

EXERCISE 2

Write out each of the following Scripture references on slips of paper or index cards: Psalm 46:1-3; Psalm 61:1-5 and Proverbs 18:10.

DISCUSSION

Due to the length of this particular lesson, you will especially need to rely on the Lord's guidance in discerning what questions to emphasize during your discussion time. Familiarize yourself with the discussion questions included in the following "Group Participation" section, or choose which questions in this week's study you want to discuss with the group.

Group Participation

EXERCISE 1

Invite those who have brought misspoken incidents to share their stories. Discuss why we tend to remember those incidents. Then share a time when someone said something about you that was hurtful. Discuss the following:

1. Why do we remember the hurtful things that others say to us?

2. How should that painful memory affect our conversations now?

3. What are some examples of things we say to people that seem innocent enough on the surface, but the person perceives them as hurtful? (*For example, nicknames, childhood taunts, not being aware of the entire situation, and so forth.*)

4. What can we do to dispel the harsh feelings that these bad memories invoke? (*Answers could include making a concerted effort to forgive that person with the help and strength of the Holy Spirit; using God's Word to replace those negative thoughts, and so forth.*)

EXERCISE 2

Give the Scripture references you wrote out on slips of paper or index cards to volunteers who are willing to read them aloud. Invite group members to share what they picture when they hear the word "peace." Most will probably share words or pictures similar to Psalm 23 (green pastures, still waters, beautiful scenery, quiet room).

Discuss when we most need God's peace (for instance, during times of stress, when bad news hits us, when we are suffering, and so forth). Next, invite the volunteers to read the following Scriptures: Psalm 46:1-3; Psalm 61:1-5; Proverbs 18:10. Discuss the following:

1. How do these verses describe the situations?

2. What are the results of running into God's strong tower?

DISCUSSION

1. As time allows, discuss the following questions (or the ones you chose) from Part One of the study:

- In Proverbs 31:26 (*NKJV*), describing the godly woman, what is your understanding of the phrase "law of kindness" (the *NIV* says "faithful instruction")?

- Can you identify with the godly woman in this verse? Why or why not?

- Read Proverbs 18:20-21. According to what you have written, in what way is the tongue responsible for life and death?

- Christians can easily fall into a habit of criticizing and judging others, thereby actually setting themselves in the place of God. According to Exodus 20:3, why is such an attitude considered so serious a sin in God's eyes?

- Read 1 John 1:9. When you do confess, what does God promise to do?

2. As time allows, discuss the following questions (or the ones you chose) from Part Two of the study:

- One aspect of the Spirit's work in us is to produce peace (see Galatians 5:22). Read Proverbs 12:20. What other fruit of the Spirit does the promoter of peace produce?

- How does trusting God enable us to yield ourselves to Him?

- Give an example of something you can do today to maintain a peaceful climate in your home and at your job.

- Read James 3:17-18. When we pray for guidance and heavenly wisdom, how do we recognize it when it comes (see verse 17)?

- What kind of harvest do peacemakers reap (see James 3:18)?

ADDITIONAL DISCUSSION/ACTION STEPS

1. Invite members to share an experience in which someone spoke the right words at the right moment. Ask them to describe how that has affected them ever since those words were spoken.

2. Invite a few volunteers to share their "listening day" experiences (see page 70).

3. Invite a volunteer or two to briefly share a time they have experienced
    God's supernatural peace in a difficulty.

End the session by having volunteers read Psalm 141:3 and Isaiah 26:3,
and then close in prayer focused on these verses.

$\mathscr{M}$INISTERING IN SUBMISSION AND HUMILITY

Objective

To help group members understand that Jesus is the model of submission and humility and that we must strive to be submissive to become more Christlike.

Preparation

EXERCISE

Obtain a lump of fresh wet clay. Take a small portion of it and set it out to dry in a shapeless lump. Keep the other half moist and in plastic until you are ready to start the lesson. Also obtain something to set the wet clay on, such as a paper plate. Bring a hammer, a flat board, a basin of water and a towel.

DISCUSSION

Familiarize yourself with the discussion questions included in the following "Group Participation" section, or choose which questions in this week's study you want to discuss with the group.

Group Participation

EXERCISE

Display the moist clay and the dried lump of clay. Discuss the differences between the two, pointing out that one is hard and the other is soft. Ask the group which of these two can be molded into a useful and/or beautiful object. (*The wet clay.*) Demonstrate that the wet clay is moldable by forming a simple little bowl, but make it lopsided. Ask, "What if this is not what I wanted this clay to look like?" (*You would work on it until it looked the way you wanted it to look.*)

Continue to work with the clay, perfecting it a little more. Don't worry if your creation is not perfect. Have some fun with it. Again ask what you would do if the clay was still not what you wanted it to look like, and then add a handle to your little bowl. Make the point that the wet clay is easy to mold into what you want it to be.

Now point to the hardened piece of clay. Ask, "Can the hardened lump be made into a useful or beautiful object? What would need to be done to make this clay moldable?" (*It would have to be broken down and soaked for a long time to be made into wet moist clay again.*)

Place the lump of clay on the board and put the towel over it. Take out the hammer and break the clay into small pieces. (*Note*: The towel is to protect group members from flying bits of clay!) Place the clay in the basin of water. It will not soften in time to show the group that it is moldable, but hopefully the group will understand that eventually it can be softened.

Ask the group how this demonstration points out the differences between a submissive spirit and a rebellious spirit. (*A submissive spirit is easier for the Master Potter to mold into the shape He can use. A rebellious spirit must be broken and soaked before it can be molded.*) Finally, ask the members which they would rather be like: the moist clay, easy to mold; or the hardened clay that needs to be broken.

DISCUSSION

Discuss the following questions (or the ones you chose) from this study:

- Everything Jesus thought, did, spoke and taught was focused toward one all-encompassing goal: to glorify God, His Father. What is the purpose, the motivation of your life at this time?

- How does it compare with Christ's goal of glorifying the Father?

- From your knowledge of God, why do you think He hates pride so much?

- What does He give the humble?

- Read Ephesians 5:22-29. What is the pattern of submission in verses 22 and 24?

ADDITIONAL DISCUSSION/ACTION STEPS

1. Ask group members what they think of when they hear the words "submission" or "humility." After a few responses for each word, ask what those in the world (our culture) think when they hear the words "submission" or "humility."

2. Discuss why many women today have such a difficult time with the concept of submitting to their husbands.

3. Ask members what are some other authorities in their lives to whom they must be submissive. (*Answers could include bosses, government, other believers, church leaders, and so forth.*)

4. Discuss what would happen if they weren't submissive to the authorities over them. (*For instance, there would be anarchy, lawlessness and chaos.*)

5. Ask the members if there is ever a time when they shouldn't be submissive to a worldly authority. Why? (*Answers could include when those authority figures ask us to do immoral acts or actions that would hurt others.*)

6. Ask why it should be easier to submit ourselves to God. (*Answers could include because He is compassionate, loving and has our best interests in mind.*)

7. Discuss why we often rebel against submitting to God.

EIGHT

MINISTERING LOVE

Objective

To help group members understand what it means to love others in the same way that God loves us—unconditionally—and to rely on the Holy Spirit who dwells within to help them love others with *agape* love.

Preparation

EXERCISE 1

On a whiteboard, chalkboard or flipchart, draw a chart with the following phrases written across the top: "*Agape* Love Is . . ." and "Even When . . ." Draw a line down the middle between the two phrases.

EXERCISE 2

Invite someone—preferably one of the group members—who could lead the group in singing two or three praise and worship songs, or obtain a worship CD and player or an MP3 player. This will be used at the end of the session. Be sure to choose two or three worship songs that focus on God's love.

DISCUSSION

Familiarize yourself with the discussion questions included in the following "Group Participation" section, or choose which questions in this week's study you want to discuss with the group. Note that if you choose to do exercise 2 above, you will want to leave about 10 to 15 minutes at the end of the session for a time of praise and worship, so choose just the number of questions that you think your group will be able to discuss during the meeting time.

Group Participation

EXERCISE 1

Invite a volunteer to read 1 Corinthians 13. Ask group members to call out the qualities of *agape* love that are listed in this passage. As they do, write their responses under the "*Agape* Love Is . . ." column. After you have listed all (or most) of the qualities, ask members to respond to the second column by suggesting things that try our *agape* love. As an example, for "patient" someone might suggest "even when a child is moving slowly on a busy day." Or for "does not envy," the suggestion might be "even when my neighbor gets a brand-new kitchen." Discuss the following questions:

1. Why is it hard to always show *agape* love?

2. What can we do to remind ourselves to love others with the same love that God shows to us?

3. How can we love someone who is difficult to love?

DISCUSSION
Discuss the following questions (or the ones you chose) from this study:

- Read 1 Corinthians 13:13. Why do you think the greatest of these is love?

- Is there a particular situation in your family (or other relationship) where a work of love needs to be accomplished in and through you? Describe what needs to be done.

- How do you react to those who have different social, moral and political views from yours?

- Read John 17:21. If the world can observe love within the Church—whose strength springs from its unity in Christ Jesus—what will be the world's ultimate realization?

- Give an example in your life in which, with God's grace, you must willfully choose to allow God's love to be expressed through you toward another person.

ADDITIONAL DISCUSSION/ACTION STEPS
1. Discuss how we can show love to our enemies or those who are hard to love. (*Answers could include by being respectful to them, by doing kind things for them, by not avoiding them, and so forth.*) Who can be considered our enemies?

2. Talk about some of the practical ways that members can show *agape* love to those they do love, such as family and friends. (*Hopefully, group members will mention many of the actions in 1 Corinthians 13.*)

3. Read John 13:34-35. Ask the members how this passage relates to the Church today. In what ways do we follow this command? In what ways has the Church failed to follow this command? What effect does the love that believers show to one another have on nonbelievers?

EXERCISE 2

Conclude this Bible study with a time of praise and worship, thanking the Lord for all He has done for the group members and especially focusing on His love for them. Begin by offering "love notes" to the Lord through a time of prayer, and then conclude with the worship songs you have chosen.

What Is Aglow International?

—◈◈◈—

From one nation to 172 worldwide...
From one fellowship to more than 4,600...
From 100 people to more than 17 million...

Aglow International has experienced phenomenal growth since
its inception 40 years ago. In 1967, four women from the state
of Washington prayed for a way to reach out to other Christian
women in simple fellowship, free from denominational boundaries.

—◈◈◈—

The first meeting held in Seattle, Washington, USA, drew more
than 100 women to a local hotel. From that modest beginning,
Aglow International has become one of the largest intercultural,
interdenominational women's organizations in the world.

—◈◈◈—

Each year, an estimated 17 million people are ministered to
through Aglow's local fellowship meetings, Bible studies, support
groups, retreats, conferences and various outreaches. From the
inner city to the upper echelons, from the woman next door to
the corporate executive, Aglow seeks to minister to the felt
needs of women around the world.

—◈◈◈—

Christian women find Aglow a "safe place" to grow spiritually
and begin to discover and use the gifts, talents and abilities God
has given them. Aglow offers excellent leadership training and
varied opportunities to develop those leadership skills.

—◈◈◈—

Undergirding the evangelistic thrust of the ministry is an emphasis on prayer, which has led to an active prayer network linking
six continents. The vast prayer power available through Aglow
women around the world is being used by God to influence
countless lives in families, communities, cities and nations.

Aglow's Mission Statement

Our mission is to lead women to Jesus Christ and provide opportunity for Christian women to grow in their faith and minister to others.

———

Aglow's Continuing Focus...

- To reconcile a woman to her womanhood as God designed. To strengthen and empower her to fulfill the unfolding plan of God as He brings restoration to the male/female relationship, which is the foundation of the home, the church and the community.
- To love women of all cultures, with a special focus on Muslim women.
- To reach out to every strata of society, from inner cities to isolated outposts to our own neighborhoods, with very practical and tangible expressions of the love of Jesus.

———

Aglow Ministers In...

Albania, Angola, Anguilla, Antigua, Argentina, Aruba, Australia, Austria, Bahamas, Bahrain, Barbados, Belarus, Belgium, Belize, Benin, Bermuda, Bolivia, Botswana, Brazil, Britain, Bulgaria, Burkina Faso, Cameroon, Canada, Chile, China, Colombia, Congo (Dem. Rep. of), Congo (Rep. of), Costa Rica, Côte d'Ivoire, Cuba, Curaçao, Czech Republic, Denmark, Djibouti, Dominica, Dominican Republic, Ecuador, Egypt, El Salvador, Equatorial Guinea, Estonia, Ethiopia, Faroe Islands, Fiji, Finland, France, Gabon, the Gambia, Germany, Ghana, Grand Cayman, Greece, Grenada, Guam, Guatemala, Guinea, Guyana, Haiti, Honduras, Hungary, Iceland, India, Indonesia, Ireland, Israel, Jamaica, Japan, Kazakstan, Kenya, Korea, Kyrgyzstan, Latvia, Lithuania, Malawi, Malaysia, Mali, Mauritius, Mexico, Mongolia, Mozambique, Myanmar, Nepal, Netherlands, New Zealand, Nicaragua, Niger, Nigeria, Norway, Oman, Pakistan, Panama, Papua New Guinea, Peru, Philippines, Portugal, Puerto Rico, Romania, Russia, Rwanda, Samoa, Samoa (American), Scotland, Senegal, Serbia, Sierra Leone, Singapore, South Africa, Spain, Sri Lanka, St. Kitts, St. Lucia, St. Maartan, St. Vincent, Sudan, Suriname, Sweden, Switzerland, Tajikistan, Tanzania, Thailand, Togo, Tonga, Trinidad/Tobago, Turks & Caicos Islands, Uganda, Ukraine, United States, Uruguay, Uzbekistan, Venezuela, Vietnam, Virgin Islands (American), Virgin Islands (British), Wales, Yugoslavia, Zambia, Zimbabwe, and other nations.

How do I find my nearest Aglow Fellowship? Call or write us at:

AGLOW
INTERNATIONAL

P.O. Box 1749, Edmonds, WA 98020-1749
Phone: 425-775-7282 or 1-800-793-8126
Fax: 425-778-9615   E-mail: aglow@aglow.org
Web site: http://www.aglow.org/

WOMEN OF THE WORD
BIBLE STUDY SERIES